Memoirs of my Childhood

Memoirs of my Childhood

St. Vincent, West Indies

Annice Browne

authorHOUSE®

AuthorHouse™
1663 Liberty Drive
Bloomington, IN 47403
www.authorhouse.com
Phone: 1-800-839-8640

First published by AuthorHouse   11/28/2011

ISBN: 978-1-4678-7835-7 (sc)
ISBN: 978-1-4678-7836-4 (ebk)

Printed in the United States of America

Any people depicted in stock imagery provided by Thinkstock are models, and such images are being used for illustrative purposes only.
Certain stock imagery © Thinkstock.

This book is printed on acid-free paper.

Contents

I dedicate this book to my family, UK born siblings, cousins, and my three daughters.

DAUGHTERS
Jasmine, Monique, Marielle
You are my greatest inspiration, and without your enthusiasm
I would not have finished this book let alone published it.
I'm so blessed to be your Mother!

Life is not about the destination, it's about the journey . . .

Acknowledgements

A special mention to my nieces and nephews from St Vincent:-

Audeene
Malc
Yonette
Mesha
Gadyon
Josh

Thank you to Auntie Claudia, Laverne, Shanelle, Colin, Malc, Ordan,
Auntie Gloria and Robert for your help and support.

Eric, thanks for your advice we talk about Jamaica and
St Vincent constantly

Childhood friends Joy and Jacqueline we share many memories; thanks for
your support and encouragement . . . it is very much appreciated!

Mum:

You are my best friend and my mentor at the end of the telephone. You have encouraged me and given me strength in difficult times. I love you unconditionally, not just because you are my mum, but because you are my soulmate.

Dad:

Love your answer-phone messages:

"Hey Annice, hope you are well; speak to you later, Daddy!" I recall when you fell ill to food poisoning, and I spoke with you on the telephone. You said: "I vomited until I could see stars!" in times of adversity, my dad still smiles. You are special to me no matter what, and I love you lots!

Foreword

This is a book of memoirs of my childhood, growing up in the Sixties, in St Vincent West Indies. My sister Polly and I were raised by our grandparents after our Mum and Dad migrated to England. Dad left in 1958, and Mum left two years later.

My UK born family comprises of three generations including siblings, cousins, and my children. In an effort to highlight the cultural differences between St Vincent and the UK, and in order to appreciate those differences, I was inspired to write this book. Furthermore, the Sixties way of life has diminished, and to record it in the form of a book is a perfect way to capture those memories!

Gran, was my paternal grandmother, and we called my maternal grandmother Mammy Darling or Grandma. My grandparents were self-employed farmers and they lived a carefree existence. They only bothered about time keeping for Sunday service and for us to attend school on time.

In the Sixties apart from public service jobs, farming life was one of the lucrative industries from which a regular income could be earned. The banana industry was the main farming trade, and most Vincentians worked smallholdings located on the hilly mountainous areas or the family garden.

Farmers who traded bananas and other vegetables earned enough to live on and funded their children's education. They also employed local people, and employees received home grown vegetables as charitable perks. Without a doubt, this gesture of goodwill provided guaranteed meals for the poor families in our community.

The diversity of backgrounds from rich to destitute was obvious to me, as the poorest families lived in wattle and daub huts with thatched roofs. It was customary for rich families to employ servants to cook and clean their homes. In spite of the poverty, when I was growing up the level of crime was low. It was safe for children and we played freely in our neighbourhood without the need for grownup supervision.

I remember from an early age my grandparents taught my sister and me that education and religion are two important requirements in life. My grandparents told me that reading books broadened the mind, they would say, education is knowledge and power. They believed that strong religious beliefs create inner strength and self-esteem. Indeed, most Vincentians knew about more modern conveniences such as electricity and pipes with running water in homes. Even without those modern amenities the women managed homes efficiently.

This book is also an opportunity for me to record my family history and my treasured memories of the grandparents who raised me. In my opinion, it's a good way to channel information about families whom our UK relatives would not have had the pleasure and honour to know. On reflection, the happy memories of my childhood, I remember carefree days of sunshine that brought exuberance to our lives.

What is greater than the mind, the poor have it, the rich don't have it, but if you don't feed it, you will die:-

Please search for my answer in one of the chapters . . .

Chapter 1

Great Grandma Malady

Childhood Inspirations—We become what we behold

My maternal great-grandma, Rosanna Harry (we called her Malady) was seventy years of age when I was born, and she was my only surviving great-grandparent. I am forever grateful for the way my grandmothers nurtured and cared for me after Mum and Dad immigrated to the England.

Grandma Malady was the leader of the family; she epitomised strength and unity. She did not fail to deliver words of wisdom. Grandma Malady believed that we must give thanks to God each day, and this ritual has stayed with me.

My great grandma was a caring person. I felt secure. She told me not be afraid of the creepy crawlies around us. It was grandma Malady that cured my fear of little green lizards, frogs, and snails. She taught me to be courageous, and I benefited from her cautionary advice.

As I sat next to her in the back garden one day, she said; "*see that tiny ant carrying a big leaf*"? We don't understand why it's carrying that big leaf. Then grandma Malady went on to say that every little creature of Mother Nature's had a purpose on Earth.

She did not finish school, but that did not prevent her from being quick-witted, and she often used to say; "*you could pick sense from nonsense*". In my opinion, if she had the opportunity to further her education, she would have been an influential woman.

What's more I often heard her say, "*education na common sense*", as she believed that a person could be coherent even without education. But I think this was the way grandma Malady dealt with her limited knowledge. At that time, illiteracy was high in St Vincent, so in a way due to the lack of education it was her common sense that played a big role in ignorance. I remember that one of her philosophical stances was that I could do anything if I was determined to succeed.

The phrases grandma Malady used were evidence of her African roots, and the way she dressed left an indelible impression on my life. Grandma Malady wore African fashions, long floral-print dresses, white cotton petticoats, and a head wrap to match—she dressed immaculately. The dresses she wore had long pockets, and she used the pockets to store food.

I imagined that during wartime, when grandma Malady was growing up, food was scarce. So, she adopted a habit of securing enough food for later. I think some of the phrases she used were from an African language she often used the word "cobbo" meaning someone was *stupid*. When my sister and I misbehaved, she used to shout, "*you cunoomonoo, a go lick yo down*". Grandma Malady never did. She often described untidy people as "kaba kaba" or "sheg-u-lay" when she argued with them.

I recall grandma Malady walked with a limp; she told me it was after a wounded toe turned septic. This happened before I was born, and as a result one of her little toes was amputated and she was left with a deformed foot. During that time, people believed in primitive obeah rituals and the casting of spells. In those days Vincentians used to believe every ailment had something to do with obeah, a type of witchcraft. She was convinced that someone had worked an obeah spell on her.

James was grandma Malady's eldest son. James lived in Trinidad at the time, and, when grandma Malady's toe turned septic, he shipped over some medicine to dress the wound. Although the medicine cured the wound, she could no longer find shoes to fit and so walked barefoot.

Grandma Malady used to tell us stories about the World wars, when there was no public transport service in St Vincent. Grandma Malady and her neighbours used to walk from Chapman's Village, setting out before dawn to go shopping in Kingstown, twelve miles away. It was a perilous journey; the roads were bumpy and covered in gravel. It was a challenge travelling by foot, a whole day return trek.

There are two songs which immediately spring to my mind when I think of grandma Malady. She often sang these verses:

> "Blessed assurance, Jesus is mine;
> Oh, what a foretaste of glory divine;
> Here are salvation, purchase of God;
> Born of his Spirit, washed in his blood;
> Come, come, oh, come, me blessed savior;
> Come, me blessed savior, sinner inna morning;
> Come, come, oh, come me, blessed savior."

At bedtime, grandma Malady sang to my younger cousins and me, and I remember the catchy lyrics.

> "Dow, dow, pity poh poh, pity poh poh, wants bread
> and milk. She would often say; Dow, dow,
> on the pillow and go to sleep."

It was a lullaby, and I'm certain she made the words up herself, but it worked a treat as we normally fell asleep after she sang to us.

At breakfast time grandma Malady loved chocolate drinks (cocoa tea) made from homegrown cocoa beans, but the drink was very rich and oily. One morning, after she drank a cup of it, she fainted. She was getting frail and old and the rich cocoa tea made her ill. I was nine years old and I thought she was dying, but after a few hours she was fit and well again.

An incident happened that I'm not proud of between grandma Malady and me. I was very mischievous and one day I climbed high into a cocoa tree in our garden. I saw her coming towards the tree. She always walked with her back slightly bent and carried a walking stick to support her. As she walked under the tree, I began to pee from where I was perched high above ground.

At first, she must have thought it was rain, but when she looked up into the tree and saw me, I knew I was in big trouble. She was furious and shouted, "*Pickney, you would get bad blessing!*" When we misbehaved, my grandparents never used physical punishment; but the words they used were effective to instil discipline. I climbed from the tree, hugged Malady, and apologised with tears in my eyes. She forgave me. My three grandmothers showered me with unconditional love, even when I was naughty. They were extremely loving and protective, and just put our misdemeanors down to childhood innocence.

Grandma Malady had many great-grandchildren. She grew frail and weak, and her sight deteriorated. Whenever her grandchildren visited her, she felt their heads to identify them. She often knew who each was from the differences in hair texture. She recognised some of my cousins, who had soft curly hair, just by touching their hair.

She often added "baby" to her grandson's names, so they were "baby Claude" for example, and it was common for her to go through a roll call of family names before she guessed the correct person. It was comical.

A few years later, grandma Malady died from a mole that turned cancerous. She passed away quietly in her sleep in the early hours of the morning at the age of eighty-four years. I have many precious memories of ten glorious years I shared with my great grandma. Her son Malcolm was a carpenter, and in those days, people had to be buried the same day they passed away because there were no mortuaries.

After grandma Malady passed away, I saw her lying in bed. She looked asleep. Later on, two women came to wash her body. Afterwards, one of the ladies sprinkled her body with talcum powder, and she was made up in a long lilac dress. Ever since that day, the smell of talcum powder reminds me of the day great-grandma Malady died.

I felt very calm after her funeral, and the period of mourning passed quickly.

Chapter 2

Midwifery Trek

My mother changed careers from a teacher to a midwife in the late Fifties, shortly after I was born. Mum was a junior nurse in the village, and the senior midwives saw her as competition. Some of the senior nurses tried to turn people against her, but as time progressed and she delivered several babies, my mum earned creditability in the community and became one of the leading midwives. Mum was on duty anytime of the day and night.

At night, it was a perilous journey without electric lights for a midwife on duty. When people called at night for Nurse Browne to assist a pregnant lady in labour, on some occasions, she travelled in total darkness with men carrying searchlights or a *flambo*. The flambo was a glass bottle filled with kerosene oil, and the wick was a long piece of cloth pushed through the bottle to soak up the oil. The flambo they carried made a perfect lamp.

Some of the night trails walking through treacherous footpaths was a challenge. Mum told us many stories about men who travelled along rugged footpaths when a wife was in labour they called at night for the midwife to go and delivery a baby. On some journeys, they had to cross rivers, and the nurse on duty would travel across the river on a donkey.

Just after our mother migrated to England, Polly and I were walking home from school. A man and his wife lived by the roadside, and as we approached their home, the husband shouted, "*yo mum garn up inna*

car". (Your mum just drove by in a car.) We believed him and hurried home, excited that our Mum was back from England. When we arrived home and told our grandma what Bankie had told us, she thought it was very malicious of him to lie to us.

At night, the kerosene lamps they used in homes had two compartments. A little drum stored the oil, and the upper compartment was a transparent, heat-resistant glass shade. A control knob turned the flame from low to high, and to turn the flame off, we just blew it out.

The old folks used to scare us with stories that jumbies (ghosts) can manifest in darkness at night. During that time, due to the lack of electricity, after 6pm everywhere was plunged into total darkness. As a consequence, I've learned to associate dark nights with supernatural life. So, my only fear was the terrifying thoughts of jumbies lurking in the darkness.

Kerosene lamp

My mother left a Singer sewing machine for my grandma, (who we called Mammy Darling), when she migrated to the England. The sewing machine was made of iron and shaped like a small table with a metal foot peddle attached to the floor. It had a right-hand wheel attached to the sewing frame. To begin stitching, grandma turned the wheel with her right hand and started peddling to sew the garment. In those days, anyone with a Singer sewing machine often set up a trade

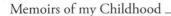

to earn money. They made clothes, cushions, pillows, pillowcases and more. Grandma regularly used sewing machine oil to keep the sewing machine from turning rusty.

My mum's brother, Rudolph Browne (Uncle Rudy), used to ride a big motorbike. In those days, a motorbike rider had almost celebrity status. Shortly before Mum travelled to England Uncle Rudy was involved in a road accident and he suffered a broken leg. Uncle Rudy was laid up in the hospital for months. I was just seven years old, and I went with Mum to visit him at the Kingstown General Hospital.

My mother didn't explain what to expect prior to visiting Uncle Rudy in hospital. I recall as I walked into the hospital ward, I saw him lying in bed with one leg elevated and pointing to the ceiling. I hadn't seen anything like it before, and I ran out of the room screaming. I had no idea what was going through my mind when I saw my uncle with one leg pointing at the ceiling. What a shocking thing it was for a seven-year-old to see, and it's amazing how trauma can stay in our sub-conscious mind.

Chapter 3

Maternal Grandmother

You Have To Be Aware Of Where You Came From—
To Appreciate Where You Are Going

I recall, every morning we woke up to the alarm sounds of what seems like hundreds of cockerels crowing at day break. It was time keeping for certain, around 6am, each day break. The poorest people who didn't have a transistor radio or alarm clock relied upon the wake up sounds.

My maternal grandmother, Mammy Darling, was five feet, three inches tall, brown skinned, with long, black, curly hair. In my opinion, she was a beautiful lady with perfectly shaped white teeth in her radiant smile. Mammy Darling had three brothers, and her parents, Rosanna Harry from Chapmans Village and Willie Browne, from Sandy Bay Village. We called the area where Mammy Darling lived "Dow-koo-tay", in Chapman's Village it is located in a valley and surrounded by mountainous hills.

Mammy Darling was a dedicated Methodist and she was always humming or singing a hymn. I often heard her say she didn't like rowdy people and preferred a quiet life. So she was friendly to everyone she knew. Mammy Darling had two daughters—my mother Bethel, and Cynthia—from her first relationship, which ended when granddad changed career to work as a sailor. By the time I was born, granddad had immigrated to America, so I only knew him by photos, but I knew his brother, great-uncle Brinsley. A few years later, grandma married Claude, and they had five children, although three survived whilst two died in their early childhood years.

Uncle Brinsley was a baker from Georgetown, and his home was in the shadow of the steep Mountain of La Soufriere volcano, but quite a distance away. When we visited Uncle Brinsley, we could see the foggy area of the mountain where the volcano lies. It looked close, but it was about four miles away up the steep mountain. If it had ever erupted, though, four miles was terrifyingly close.

I was four years old, and our extended family had increased. I had a few more cousins and we lived in an overcrowded home, but we were one big happy family. Most homes had galvanized tin roofs, and when it rained, especially at night in bed, the pitter-patter of raindrops on the roof helped me to relax. It was incredibly tranquil. Every morning, I heard hundreds of cockerels begin crowing loudly at daybreak. We did not need an alarm clock to wake us and the cockerels crowing to mark the beginning of each day.

The land surrounding our home had various fruit trees, but mostly banana trees. They grew to be over ten feet high. This made the yard very dark, especially at night. We had no electricity, and the only natural light outdoors was when the moon shone at night. Every day, people used to go to nearby rivers in order to collect water. Grandma routinely filled a big, galvanized tub with water to use for baths the next morning. There was also an area where we could fetch clean drinking spring water, and the family always boiled the water we drank.

Prior to bath time every morning, grandma boiled a pot of water and poured it into the tub of cold water to make it lukewarm to take the chill off when she gave me a bath. To keep my hair clean, grandma used the liquid of a fresh prickly pear. It cleaned my scalp and left my hair shiny.

Our breakfast wasn't lavish; it was bread and butter with drinking chocolate or coffee. The drinks were freshly grounded cocoa and coffee beans from the family garden mixed with fresh cow or goat's milk. At breakfast we had some of the eggs our hens laid; the eggs were boiled or fried—depending on whether grandma had cooking oil. We also ate farine for our breakfast cereal. We used milk or soaked the farine in tea. The farine cereal was made from cassava, a starchy root vegetable that was sun dried, grated, and then baked in a hot oven. Grandma made other hot drinks she called black tea. The selections were peppermint, ginger, fever grass, guinea pepper. We had whatever was available, and we did not complain.

My grandparents had a few nanny goats that produced milk which they then sold to the neighbours. Gran also tried to make goats cheese, but failed. For breakfast on some occasions, my grandmother boiled milk and added a little mint leaf to make mint-flavoured milk tea. We also enjoyed cornmeal porridge. The cornmeal was made from corn harvested from our family garden and it was a hot and filling milky meal. To make the cornmeal, the green corn on the cobs were first sun-dried and then finely ground into flour. It was a cumbersome task, as our grandparents ground the corn manually using a machine and churned the handle for hours.

When grandma made cornmeal porridge she would add goat's or cow's milk, a bay leaf, cornmeal flour, sugar to a pan, and constantly stir the ingredients so that the porridge did not form lumps. She let it simmer for twenty minutes and the porridge thickened. It made a delicious meal that we ate as a snack any time of day. The cornmeal was also used in various dishes; we enjoyed cornmeal bread and fried bakes. In different Caribbean islands, the latter is also known as johnny cakes, fried dumplings, or festivals.

The daily morning chores after breakfast consisted of moving the livestock from their night shelters to graze in the fields for the day. Likewise, farm workers would set off to their fields to tend vegetable crops. They did general gardening duties, ploughing, and weeding all day long. They even made fires and cooked meals on their lunch breaks. Women with young children stayed at home, though some worked as dressmakers, while other women were busy preparing their crops for market.

The women spent hours collecting oranges, limes, lemons, and grapefruits, and packing them for wholesale on market stalls. It was a long and laborious task to prepare coffee beans, cocoa beans, nutmeg, and coconuts for market. The beans all needed to be picked, stripped, peeled, shelled, and then sun-dried it took a few weeks for the product to be completed for sale. The cocoa beans grew in a large capsule and, when fully grown, they turned golden yellow or red.

The cocoa beans covered in a sweet white coating, and attached to something the old folks called the cocoa heart. The cocoa heart was edible, and when I was growing up, we used to suck the white covering off the cocoa beans and we ate the white, edible cocoa heart. The fresh picked beans needed to be sun-dried after the beans were sun-dried they were ready to be parched and milled into chocolate. My grandmothers used a big copper pot to roast the beans over a high heat. As soon as the cocoa beans were parched enough, they used a mortar and pestle to grind the roasted beans. The mortar looked like a big concrete bucket, and the concrete pestle was shaped like a baseball bat so it was quite heavy.

She spent hours pounding and grinding the cocoa beans until they turned into thick, gluey, chocolate dough. She shaped the chocolate dough into chocolate sticks then left them to dry and harden. To make drinking chocolate, grandma grated the chocolate sticks into boiling water and added milk and sugar to taste. She also earned a bit of money selling the sticks of chocolate to her neighbours.

Breadfruit season was similar to summertime barbecues. My grandmothers often roasted breadfruits outdoors on an open wood fire. Breadfruit can be roasted, cooked, or fried, and there are two types of breadfruit. The cream flesh breadfruit is perfect for roasting, and the white flesh breadfruit is suitable for casserole meals.

Roasted breadfruit is delicious with fried fish, pork, or beef stew. In other dishes, thinly sliced breadfruit is deep-fried to make savoury dishes such as crisps and chips. During the breadfruit harvest, when grandma needed to pick breadfruit from the tree, she used a long pole with a sharp knife tied to the top end. I used to get very excited when grandma planned to pick breadfruits. Polly and I often went along with grandma carrying the long pole with a sharp knife securely tied at the end.

My sister and I carried a basket or a crocus bag to collect the breadfruits and some grow singly or about three in a bunch. Grandma stood firmly on the ground holding the long pole then chose a breadfruit the size of a watermelon. Then she placed the sharp knife behind the breadfruit stem and drew the knife forward to cut the breadfruit from its branch. We stood at a distance beneath the tree to collect the falling breadfruit. The women also used this method to pick various fruit that hung high in the trees.

The breadnut is like the chestnut available in the UK. The breadnut and it is always in season in St Vincent; it can be boiled or roasted, and when they are boiled, they make a delicious snack hot or cold. Breadnut boiled and soaked in salt makes a delicious, savoury side dish or snack. The breadnut tree looks like the breadfruit tree, but the fruit grows like a big green ball with several nuts inside. A grown breadnut is like a prickly green ball containing several nuts similar to chestnuts.

Breadfruit plant

Our grandmothers often made guava jam, which was delicious spread on bread. They used the ripe guavas, about sixteen ounces, sliced, de-seeded, and boiled in water. Then they added sixteen ounces of brown sugar and simmered it for two hours until the guavas and sugar turned to a thick paste.

My other favourite side dish was mashed ripe *zaboka* (avocado) mixed with farine. Ripe avocados can also be used in sandwiches or added to salads. During the summertime, zaboka was plentiful. Gran and Mammy Darling prepared the farine and zaboka mixture for us to eat as a snack. When the zaboka is smashed with farine, the mixture is a lovely green colour. At dinnertime, we rolled the mixture into little balls as a side dish or spread it on bread. We had a big, sturdy avocado tree in our garden, and every summer Grandma earned a bit of money selling avocados. Avocados, when fully grown in St Vincent, are the size of a grapefruit and some stay green even when ripe. Others turn deep burgundy red.

The tropical weather and fertile volcanic soil in St Vincent is perfect for growing vegetables and most people turned the land surrounding their homes into profitable farms. Most landowners harvest enough produce to sell at market and earn enough money to live on. St Vincent produces a high volume of vegetables and sells to neighbouring islands, trading these by boat to the faraway islands of Trinidad and Jamaica.

In my opinion, I learned how to be resourceful by planting and harvesting vegetables in our family garden. One summer, my sister and I planted peas and sweet corn in our family garden and watched them grow. We had planted three types of peas—pigeon peas, green peas, and calico peas. We watered them first thing every morning, before the sun got hot. A few months later, when the peas and corn were fully grown, we often sat with Gran shelling peas and ate roasted corn.

A Person Who Came From Nowhere Can Go Anywhere

It was difficult for our grandmothers to prepare meals each day. They used the most basic appliances to cook meals. Every day, they had to make up either an open wood fire or coal pot fire, and it took more than an hour to prepare supper from start to finish. After striking the match, they had to fan the wood or coals repeatedly to spread the sparks. As soon as I was old enough, it was one of my chores to help grandma make a fire. I remember how the smoke burnt my eyes and sometimes I blew the sparks until I felt dizzy.

The coal pot our family used was made of cast iron. It had two compartments. The upper shelf stored the coals or wood, and the metal pot sat on a stand with an open vent. The top shelf of the coal pot had grid holes for the ashes to escape. When the coal pot was in use, the hot ashes created the prefect oven for baking sweet potatoes, tanias, bananas, and plantains, to name a few. In my opinion, the coal pot is the best appliance for roasting breadfruit and even today modern ovens take second place.

Every evening, smoke billowed in the sky around the villages. From a distance, as people travelled home from work in the evening, they often said that they knew exactly when dinner was being cooked as the smoke went from grey to a bluish-grey.

From Small Beginnings Come Great Things

In those days, for fire safety reasons, it was high risk to combine the living room and kitchen. An open fire was too dangerous, but by the mid-sixties, a cleaner cooking appliance went on sale and more and more people including my grandmothers had purchased stoves. The stoves were cleaner and easy to operate. A stove operated from a gas cylinder or oil barrel required just an on/off switch and a match to ignite the flames. This was a quicker way to prepare a meal, but it was costly to replace the oil or gas and not everyone could afford to maintain them, so quite a few people still used a coal pot or open fire to cook meals.

Coal Pot

During my childhood, only the very rich (less than half the population) lived in large, stand-alone houses. Other homes had three separate buildings. One housed the living room (grandma called it "the hall") and bedrooms. The other two separate buildings were a kitchen and a latrine. In those days most Vincentians used a latrine. It was a smaller building which housed a cesspit covered by a wooden floor and a commode box with lid. At night, people used a chamber pot (pooh) kept under their beds. They emptied the chamber pot down the cesspit every morning and cleaned the chamber pot with disinfectant daily.

An inspector employed by the government visited the villages regularly. He often checked the latrines to ensure people were maintaining good hygiene standards. When grandma saw the inspector approaching our home, she would shout loudly, "kaka inspector a-come!" (The inspector is coming!)

There was a stigma attached to the role of latrine inspector, people regard it as a demeaning job to do. But stigma or not, it was an important role and necessary to teach people how to maintain basic hygiene. The latrine inspector taught us to always wash our hands after using the sanitary cubicle.

Every week, sometimes daily, a van drove by on the main road selling fresh fish, and the fishmonger blew on a big seashell to alert villagers. As soon as we heard the shell, grandma went to the main road to buy fresh fish. However, grandma did not believe that children should purchase fresh fish, as it was important to know the difference between fresh or stale fish. We learned what to look for in a fresh fish. If the eyes of the fish looked bloody, according to grandma, they were stale.

The van that drove around the villages selling fish stored them in wicker baskets without ice. To keep the fish fresh, the fishmonger needed a quick sale. The selection included small sprat fish, and the larger red snapper or tuna. There was a medium-sized fish called *balaou*. It had a long spike attached to its mouth, and the spike was as tough as metal.

Most people purchased bread from a bread van daily. As soon as I was old enough, I would go to the main road to buy a dozen small rolls of bread from the bread van. The baker always gave a "baker's dozen" (thirteen bread rolls), but I was crafty and considered it my reward. I used to eat the extra bread roll on my way home. Grandma didn't suspect any wrongdoing. A few years later, the Sunrise bakery van drove through villages and sold various cakes to the local shops.

We had a local baker and he only baked bread on the weekends and special occasions, for example wedding orders. He used an oven made from wattle and daub (similar in design to an Eskimo igloo) and heated with wood or coals. The baker used big metal trays, and a long flat piece of wood to lift the trays in and out of the heated oven.

A Candle Loses Nothing If It Is Used To Light Another One

Auntie Cynthia, grandma's second daughter, was a sick lady. I was told that she had a hole in her heart. Auntie Cynthia lived in Trinidad for several years and returned home because of ill health. When I was young, I often wondered if anyone could survive with a hole in his or her heart. Auntie Cynthia was on medication. She took a tiny tablet called finabob. Some days she was well, and other days she was weak and shaky. She had a strong voice but a weak body and went out of breath when she walked a short distance. Auntie Cynthia was a dark, skinny lady, quite tall—about 5ft 9ins—and her hair was very long, especially the front. It reached her chest, but the back was much shorter.

Auntie styled her hair by wrapping the front with a side part and scraping the hair to one side around the back of her head. A big gap separated her two top front teeth. She didn't have children of her own, so she treated me as hers. She bought me a lovely red felt hat from Trinidad and often styled my hair. I went to Uncle Eric's (Mammy Darling's brother) wedding, and Auntie Cynthia styled my hair. I felt very grown up. She even allowed me to wear her lipstick. In those days, not a lot of people had cameras, and there were no photos of the wedding. Auntie Cynthia died at age thirty-seven in 1971. God rest her soul.

~*~*~*~*~

There Are Many Things In Your Life That Will Catch Your Eye,
But Only A Few Will Touch Your Heart

Mammy Darling had a clever way to warn me to stay away from teenage boys. She sang a song. The song goes:

> *"Monday morning me bin fo water;*
> *Meet John wid a roll a cocoa;*
> *Beg John fo piece e cocoa;*
> *John say e full a pepper;*
> *John yo lie yo na war fo gimme."*

Still very young and naïve, I did not understand the lyrics until I was a teenager. The message is similar to the sexual undertone of most calypso lyrics. In those days, sexuality was a taboo subject. Our grandmothers' strict rules prevented them from talking to us about sex. Our grandmothers did not teach us about puberty or what to expect when we started menstruating; we were told by older schoolmates.

Our aunts taught us to sing:

> *"Oh, Miss Cane she had a baby;*
> *And she laid it in the grass;*
> *And the grass e catcha fire;*
> *E burn e burn the baby to rag;*
> *Oh e burn e burn ah baby to rag."*

When the old folks were busy chatting and sex was mentioned, they told us it was an adult conversation and often replaced a person's name with slang words. On numerous occasions, the old folks told us: *"you must not interrupt adult conversation, and children must speak when spoken to"*.

My sister and I often walked in on grandma and her friends chitchatting, grandma didn't want us to repeat what we heard so they would replaced a person's name with slang words, such as *"say-k; bay-k"*, and other coded words. They could not fool us though as Polly and I

often guessed who they were gossiping about. It was interesting for us as we sat and listened while grandma and her friends thought that it was safe to talk that way, they agreed we were just innocent children. But I now realise that one of the most destructive forces in the universe is idle gossip.

Progress Has Little To Do With Speed,
But Much To Do With The Direction We Chose

Mammy Darling had over two dozen chickens. As soon as it was six p.m., they all flew up into one of the cocoa trees in our garden. Grandma only kept the young chickens in a cage because they were too young to fly. It was strange that the chickens had a bedtime routine and there was a mass exodus every evening. During the day, when there was a storm brewing, the hens and cockerels often looked bemused and the hens would take shelter and gathered chicks under their bodies.

Grandma had a big cockerel who was king of the flock, but a thief came one night and stole him. Later on, there was news going around the village that the man who stole the cockerel was bragging about filling his pot with meat. At the time, I was very upset, as I treated the chickens like pets and I fed them every day with grains of corn. I was very attached to them. Grandma often asked me to buy special feed from the shop; the shop sold growina, and layina, the former for young chickens and the latter to help hens produce eggs.

Children, when they were not at school, needed to be aware of dark clouds and alert their parents. Farmers made use of the good weather and sun-dried the cocoa, coffee beans, nutmeg, and coconuts for market. Dark clouds in St Vincent meant rain. The dark clouds formed at the seacoast, and the old folks used to say, "Rain set up." The dark clouds worked their way inland, followed by rain. However, it was normally just showers, and the earth soaked up the water quickly. Grandma had two nutmeg trees and she sold the seeds and mace. Nutmeg grows in a cream capsule, and as soon as the nutmeg seeds are ready for harvesting, the capsules burst open, showing the red mace.

The nutmeg seed is enclosed in a shell, and the mace covering the shell looks like knitted pattern of red thread. It was a laborious task to harvest nutmegs and it took weeks to prepare them for market. I had to help grandma as soon as I was old enough—about seven. We had to strip the nutmeg capsules to reach the mace and seed, and then remove the mace from the seed, which was covered by a hard shell. The dried nutmeg seeds and mace were sold and exported to the UK, America, and Canada. Both are used in a variety of menus.

I quickly learned the value of money and often climbed the nutmeg trees to collect enough nutmeg to sell. I will never forget the day when I climbed a nutmeg tree I stretched to reach a nutmeg I slipped and fell from the tree. Lucky for me, I landed on soft ground and suffered no broken bones, but I bashed my head. I suffered a slight concussion, and it affected my hearing for some time afterwards. After my fall, Mammy Darling gave me a thick, bitter liquid made from the aloe vera plant. She told me it could repair internal bruises. She held a sweet in one hand and the drink in the other hand. A few minutes later, she persuaded me to drink the bitter liquid and then I ate the sweet to get rid of the bitter taste. Grandma was right; I felt better within a few days.

Most people do not realise that the coconut is a versatile fruit. The coconut is not just used for sweet snacks, but as an ingredient for a wide variety of dishes and toiletries. When the coconut is sun dried, it is called *copra*. The coconut is used to extract oil for an ingredient in shampoos, body lotions, hair care creams, and soaps. Even the outer skin, husks, and shells are used to make fire.

The green coconut contains a soft white flesh inside, and it looks like jelly (hence the name "coconut jelly"). It is picked fresh from the tree and ready to eat. The coconut contains water. I think it is a delicious drink, but not everyone agrees with me coconut water is an acquired taste. Coconuts hang high up in the trees until they turn brown and the stem goes dry, and then they fall from the tree. The dried coconuts are used in various meals, and there are many recipes containing coconut. It was a cumbersome task preparing coconuts for market; the process took weeks of hard labour.

My grandmothers used to extract coconut milk from coconuts by grating the flesh then adding a little water, and squeezing the flakes through a sieve or a strainer. Gran often made delicious fudges using the coconut milk by boiling it with brown sugar and other ingredients. To extract oil, she boiled the coconut milk.

My dear beloved grandmother (Mammy Darling) was born in 1912 and she passed away in 1996 at the age of eighty-four.

Chapter 4

Paternal Grandparents

Happy Families Are Like Angels Who Lift Us To Our Feet
When Our Wings Have Trouble Remembering How To Fly

Our grandparents were Samuel and Mary Cupid (Gran), a family of two sons and a daughter, my dad, Avil, Uncle Lester, and Auntie Claudia. After our parents immigrated to England, my sister and I enjoyed the best of both homes our paternal and maternal grandparents cared for us. I was five years old when Dad travelled to England.

Obviously, my paternal grandparents were special to my sister and me. Granddad wasn't openly affectionate like Gran, but Polly and I knew we were special to him. We were raised in an orderly Christian home, and Gran planned our upbringing efficiently.

During school holidays, every morning after breakfast she used to braid our hair. We wore clean clothes every day. Gran didn't allow us to play outdoors wearing school uniforms or our Sunday clothes; we dressed appropriately. Gran was an excellent seamstress. I remember she made me my favourite red check dress with pockets; it had a belt she made from the same fabric.

She was an extremely good cook, very creative in the kitchen. Gran made all types of snacks. Her meals weren't boring. She made sweet and savory snacks, such as cassava bread and many flavours of fried dumplings. When Gran made coconut sugar cakes, Polly and I helped. We used a knife and a big bowl and sliced the coconut flesh into small pieces.

Almost every weekend on school holidays, she made fudges and coconut sugar cakes. These were our special treats, and I used to get very excited when it was time for Gran to make us sweeties.

Granddad took the role of father to Polly and me, though I felt that he couldn't replace Dad. Our granddad was a very strict disciplinarian, unlike Dad, who was more fun loving and affectionate. We normally ate Sunday meals sitting at the dining table and granddad told us it was bad manners to put our elbows on the table, and after so many decades, this still comes back to haunt me. When I am dining with friends, I unconsciously place my elbows on the table, and the moment I realise what I've done I immediately remove my elbows, as if granddad is watching me. I honestly believe that some of what we experience and learn during our formative years sets like concrete in our subconscious minds.

Our families owned acres of lands farming fruits, vegetables, pigs, goats, and chickens. Granddad employed a few people to help with the banana plantation. They gave names to their farmlands, too. My grandparents owned Julie Gutter, and Crown land in separate locations, plus a huge vegetable garden around our home. Every morning, Gran carried the goats out to the field to graze and used a stake to tie the goats' leads to stop them from roaming off her land. One day, one of the goats slipped over the cliff and hung itself by the rope.

Gran kept the goats in the basement at night, which was an open shelter. Steps at the side of the house led to the basement. One day, Polly and I heard the groans of a nanny goat coming from the basement, so we went to investigate. I had never seen anything like it before, and I thought the nanny goat was dying. My Gran saw us.

She shouted, "*come away from there; alyo too young to see that*," but we were already in full view by then. Actually, the goat was in labour, and I think it was an appropriate time for Gran to explain the birds and the bees. We were too shy to ask questions, but we understood later when we saw the new kiddy goat.

During school holidays, every morning after breakfast, Gran sat for an hour to braid our hair then we showered. The shower room was in the basement, and we used a big galvanized container filled with lukewarm water. Sometimes we went to the fields with Gran and sat under a shaded tree looking on while the workers ploughed and weeded the vegetable patches. At mid-day, when the sun was too hot, we stayed indoors, playing with our dolls or listening to the radio. I used to irritate my sister with practical jokes and would often repeat everything she said. It was mischievous and lively for me, and I used to relish her reaction.

Gran kept a few pigs in a pigpen. She often asked Polly and me to scratch their bellies, but the pigpen was smelly and dirty. I loathed the touch of the pigs' bellies, as they felt hairy and grainy. When Gran wasn't looking, I would pretend that I was assisting the pigs, but I used to just wait outside the pigpen. The pigs needed help scratching their bellies because they were too short to use a tree when they needed a good scratch.

We ate home raised chickens for Sunday dinner, and granddad didn't hesitate to pick one of our pets. He held the chicken by the neck, placed it on a chunk of wood, and chopped the head off. I know exactly what it means when the old folk say, "*you are jumping around like a headless chicken*", because that is what used to happen when granddad killed a chicken.

Only Fools Laugh At Their Own Calamity

The headless chicken remained alive for a few minutes, jumping around, and then Gran plucked the feathers off while the body was still warm. She told us it was easier to remove the feathers then. It was normal, but I think today, I wouldn't be able to watch the demise of a chicken for my meal.

Granddad was a tall, handsome, very strict disciplinarian. One day, he asked Polly and me to hold open a crocus bag so that he could fill the bag with coconut shells. In my view when situations get too orderly, it tended to spark laughter. I began to laugh, and even though Polly had no idea what the joke was, it was so infectious she began to laugh. I laughed uncontrollably couldn't stop myself and I peed my pants, the wet flowing down my legs was obvious. Granddad was so annoyed he remarked, "*damn it; only fools laugh at their own calamity.*" At the time, I wondered what calamity meant and it was a new word I'd learned and the word calamity always reminds me of that incident many years ago.

We listened to the radio broadcasting the *BBC World Service News* every evening at home. On Saturday night, when the football pool results were announced, my sister and I would guess the results of the games. The results tended to reverse between "nil" and "three." Polly and I played a game guessing the correct results. Even though we didn't understand what was being announced over the radio, we made good use of that program. Many years later, I realised the announcements were the British football game results played earlier that day. After the football results were announced, the shipping forecasts followed, and at the time I remembered, "*what is altitude and longitude?*"

Granddad had a big grey donkey. He used it to transport him to his farmland and carried heavy produce. One day, I climbed onto the donkey while my sister held a rope attached to the donkey's neck. She pulled the donkey sternly, and the donkey raced off. I fell, and my foot got stuck in the stirrup. I was dragged through gravel and was scared for my life.

Saturday was laundry day. Polly and I often accompanied Gran to wash clothes in the river. This was long before water pipes were connected in homes. We often looked forward to laundry day, as we met up with other families at the river. Some of the ladies took time to fish for crabs and crayfish and would often cook a meal by the riverbank on an open fire.

The women would dam off part of the river and lay big stones across it from one end to the other that wall obstructed the flow of water. Then the women filled the gap between the stones with soil and weeds. This stopped the rapid flow of water escaping behind the dam stones. The shallow water behind the wall made it easier to catch the crabs, crayfish, and mullets. We could see everything all the fish panicked through the crystal clear shallow water. I enjoyed catching crayfish, but the crabs used to bite, and the mullets were too slippery to grab.

After the ladies caught enough, they cleaned the fish with lime or lemon juice. For flavour, they marinated them with chives and coconut milk. The women used three big stones to seat the pot and dried twigs or coconut husks to make a fire. They added crabs, mullets, and crayfish to a mix of sweet potatoes or yams and dumplings that made a casserole. A delicious, hot meal simmered while the women hand-washed their laundry.

On laundry day, when Gran rinsed the clothes, she dipped them into a starchy liquid. The starch made it easier to iron the white cotton shirts and blouses. Gran often used sunlight soap or breeze soap powder, as well as clorox liquid bleach to remove stains. Gran believed the hot sun could bleach stains from soiled white clothes.

After washing the garment in soapy water, she left the wet, soapy clothes bunched together in the hot sun for a half hour. This made it easier to scrub the stains away. Gran often rinsed my white blouses for school by dipping them in a bluey liquid so my blouses looked brand new and bluey white with every wash.

For ironing, people used heavy cast-irons and the coal pot fire to heat them. Half an hour before grandma began ironing she sprinkled the clothes with water and folded them neatly. The damp clothes made it easier to iron out creases. It worked exactly like an electric stem iron. She placed the cast-irons on the coal pot fire for at least thirty minutes before she began ironing. When an iron was hot enough, grandma used it until it cooled down. With three irons heating up at the same time, she had constant hot irons to use.

My grandmothers had three irons. In those days, there was no ironing board and grandma used the dining table and covered it with old sheets. Just before grandma began ironing the clothes, she would wipe the hot iron with a clean cloth to be certain there was no trace of black coal on the iron.

Your Eyes Are The Windows Of Your Soul

The views from my grandparents' house were stunning. We could see the surrounding areas overlooking hills and mountains miles away in the distance. At my grandparents' home the front door faced south overlooking nearby villages of Lowman's Windward, Gregg's Hill, bordering Maroon Hill, they were all panoramic views from home. At the north-side mountain views, hills, and valleys. The mountains often looked blue-grey on sunny days. To the east, my other grandmother (Mammy Darling) lived across a river. On a bright sunny day, the views from home were a spectacular picture of luscious greenery, mostly banana plantations. On a bright, sunny, clear blue sky day, the sea looked turquoise, and from that distance of four miles, the waves formed twinkling stars. As I looked towards the sea, it gave me the impression that the sea's horizon joined with the sky.

One day, Polly and I saw a big ship sailing by, and my Gran told us it was from England. Occasionally, we saw a big cruise ship anchored a few miles offshore overlooking San Souci village; Gran told us the ship crew were emptying their waste—dumping shit in our sea water. My sister and I stood on the hill near our home waving at the ship. I imagined people using their binoculars to watch villagers as they go about their business.

In Chapman's Village, where I lived, bordered New Adelphi on the east side, and beyond that New Grounds, bordering Diamond's Village, and I thought it was the world, my world, until I learned geography in school. The panoramic of the villages around me was similar to watching a television show. I saw people nearby, and some at a distance, going about their daily chores.

I saw people with heavily laden donkeys, and some with cattle, goats, and flock of sheep especially late evening when they were taking stock to night shelters.

During school holidays and on weekends, I stayed with my paternal grandparents with my sister Polly. The house surrounded a huge garden with fruit trees and a variety of vegetable crops. During the month of August mangoes and other fruits were in season. Waking up to brilliant sunshine felt good, and my sister and I used to create our own entertainment during the day.

Dad left an accordion, and my sister and I used to play it when Granddad was busy working in his garden. As we played with the accordion, I didn't understand music, but I realised if I pressed the black and white keys, sound would play. One day, Granddad came home early and caught us using the accordion Dad had left. We were ordered not to touch it again.

Granddad was eager to protect our dad's belongings after he migrated to the England. Granddad also told us that Dad used to play the accordion at Sunday service. He told Polly and me that listening to Dad performed in church it "*swelled his nose*." This was Granddad's way of describing how proud he was when Dad played the accordion in church.

Polly had a doll we named "Darling". It was a unique doll, as the head was porcelain, and its body part was made of cloth. I was very fond of that doll as it was flexible and we could move its arms and legs like a real baby. The porcelain head was sewn to its cloth body, which made it easy to bend.

During that time, Mum was living in the England, and we received parcels with lots of new clothes, toys, biscuits, and toffees on a regular basis. I received a doll from England that walked when I wound it up with a key, and we named it Rosebud, the name was printed on the doll's back. Our cousin Yvonne made some lovely little intricate dresses for our dolls; they were some of the best-dressed dolls in our village.

A few years later, when my sister started Emmanuel High School in Kingstown, our Gran burnt all of our dolls and other toys. I was devastated. The wrench was just as bad as the time we watched our puppy die. Gran told us it was time to buckle down with our studies as it cost money to attend secondary school.

One day, Gran cooked cornmeal-coo for supper, Polly and I didn't like the taste. Gran tried to force us to eat the cornmeal-coo, but we gave it to the dog. The dog's name was Croga. It was a big brown dog that belonged to Auntie Claudia. Gran took the dog in when Auntie Claudia migrated to England. Even the dog refused to eat the cornmeal-coo. Croga just walked away and left the cornmeal-coo in full view for Gran to see. It was the only fault of Gran's cooking, as she was an excellent cook. She made delicious coconut toffees she called fudge. My Gran's cassava bread was the best I had tasted. She also made lovely fried bakes (fried dumplings) of many flavours—coconut, cornmeal, and ma-dong-o—all delicious.

No Good Turn That Is Not Appreciated Goes Unpunished

One day, Polly and I went to our neighbour. They were eating supper with a guest. The elderly lady offered us food from her plate, and we took the food, said goodbye, and then dumped the food by the gate. A young man who was walking by saw what we did and told the old lady. She was very offended and complained to our granddad.

Granddad told us off and explained to us that the neighbours were poor, and if we didn't want the food that was offered to us, we should have politely refused it. My sister and I knew that we were at fault, and I learned a valuable lesson—"*waste not, want not.*" Nowadays I'm more cautious of food waste and routinely use stale bread to make bread pudding. Any leftover food is kept in the fridge and reheated for a meal the next day. Even though we offended that poor old lady, it taught me a valuable lesson.

We had a front garden with a big green lawn surrounding our house and the lawn always looked tidy. The nanny goats used to maintain the lawn as my grandparents didn't have a lawn mower. The garden had several colours of gerberas, roses, and red hibiscus, and another flowers plant. My sister and I often picked the blossoms off to make necklaces. The lawn was a perfect play ground my sister and I sometimes spun around in circles until it made us dizzy.

We had a pet cat, and she had four kittens. Gran kept the kittens in a cardboard box down the garden shed, where she kept sweet potatoes, yams, and green corn on the cob she'd hung in the hut to dry. Kittens are born blind, and they were just a few days old—tiny, hairless, and feeble—I remember they could only move their heads from side to side. I was petrified of the helpless kittens and just couldn't bear to look at them. A few months later, they were adorable, fluffy, black and white kittens, and Gran found homes for all of them.

Granddad built some shelves in the garden shed the shelves were planks of wood which stretched across the ceiling. The planks

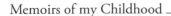

stretched from one end of the ceiling to the other so it made overhead ledges big enough for children to hide on. One day, we saw granddad heading towards the shed, and Polly and I decided to play a practical joke on him.

We told our cousin Mark to hide on one of the shelves. Granddad walked in, and Mark started meowing like a cat. Granddad thought he had stepped on the cat and looked down fearing he might have hurt her. Polly and I began to laugh, and when granddad looked up and saw Mark hiding on the ledge, he was not amused!

Gran had a dressing table with a big mirror in her bedroom on which she kept perfumes and other cosmetics on display. I was about seven or eight years old and was curiously searching through everything on the dressing table. One by one, I sniffed all of the fragrances.

I came across a tiny bottle of smelling salts and unscrewed the top. It had a removable plastic seal, so I pulled it off. The moment I opened the bottle, a strong smell whiffed across my eyes, but I ignored it. I took a deep sniff of the smelling salts, and the aroma travelled up my nostrils, straight to my brain. I was traumatised with pain. My eyes went runny, my nose went red, and I knew from that bad experience that smelling salts was power in a tiny bottle. My sister Polly told me that smelling salts was for big people, and I had to avoid it, as it wasn't safe for children.

Chapter 5

Adventures

Live Life To The Fullest, Laugh Often,
And Love With Your Whole Heart

In an effort to keep children happy and active, it was necessary for parents to make good use of their inventiveness. Carpenters made toys, swings, and go-carts. Some of the toys children used to play with were imaginative, too, as boys used old vehicle wheels as toys. They used a stick to navigate the wheel by placing the stick on the outer circle of the wheel and running along the tarmac, rolling the wheel. Sometimes a few boys raced to see who was faster. Some children had homemade go-carts; the entire cart was made of wood, even the wheels.

We played many games that kept us physically fit—especially skipping rope games. I suppose that in every school playground in the world, skipping rope is common. I am certain everyone would agree with me that skipping games requires concentration. I quickly learned the technique of jumping in the center of a spinning rope as I evolved further skills. This level of skipping requires good coordination to guess when to run clear before the rope spun mid-way to the ground.

The more advanced levels were played with multiple players. Up to six of us skipped together. As the rope spun, we took turns jumping out from the spinning rope; the person who got caught in the rope lost the game. I played many skip rope games after school. We used to sing while we skipped. The song goes:

There's a brown girl in the ring;
Char-la-la-la-la;
There's a brown girl in the ring;
Char-la-la-la-la;
A brown girl in the ring;
Char-la-la-la;
She looks like sugar inna plum; plum, plum;

Just before the singing stopped, a player ran from the spinning rope, if you stopped the rope from spinning, you lost the game. We played until there were no more players. We also played relay race. Each player stood behind a line and the games referee shouted, "*on your mark, get set, go*". One of my school friends, Cynthia Richards, was the fastest runner. She was strong, and if it were today, she would be a world-class Olympic runner. We also played hopscotch. It was part of our daily exercise.

We played hopscotch with pebbles, and it was some of the most enjoyable playtime I can remember. After school and on weekends, the only time we spent indoors was to shelter from the hot mid-day sun. I remember August being the hottest; the weather was always humid and sticky. I looked like a burnt lobster and my hair went from brown to red.

Marble games were mainly for boys, but I was always willing to take part in any challenges that came my way. The marble game is similar to playing snooker. We bunched several marbles together then each player used a bigger marble to try to hit the marbles from a distance. At the initial opening, the aim is to separate the marbles.

The second step for a single marble: if you hit the target, you play until you missed. When we played, the person who hit the most marbles won the game and kept the marbles.

Frequently, we played rounders and cricket. For a ball, we used young limes or lemons picked from the trees in our garden or a neighbour's garden. When we played cricket, we made the bat and wickets from old pieces of wood. We had two types of lemons growing in our garden. One type the family sold, and the other type was excellent for scrubbing floors. We were allowed to use as many of the household cleaning lemons to play our ball games but not the other type of lemons our grandparents sold.

We used gravel to play hopscotch and skittle dash. In skittle dash, we piled a dozen pebbles in a pyramid, and each player took turns using a small bouncing ball. To start the game, the player bounced the ball on the ground and when the ball was thrown in mid-air the player quickly grabbed a pebble. If the player succeeded without crashing the bunch of pebbles, the player continued to play until the pebble pyramid crashed. The player can also aim to grab pebbles; the more you can grab, the quicker you can win the game.

One day my sister Polly and I, and our cousins Wilma and Dandy, were travelling through our neighbour's garden something we enjoyed during playtime. We saw a rope hanging from a huge cedar tree. It was typical to find wild vines like long rope growing from some of the big old trees. The rope was long enough to reach the ground, but the rope wasn't safe. It was bark growing from the tree. I suppose back then we were young and naïve. It looked exactly like strong thick rope.

We decided to use the rope as a swing and took turns holding onto it while the others pushed the person holding the rope out for a ride. There were no playgrounds in those days, so I suppose we used to create our own playtime ventures, notably the cedar rope game. We didn't take time to consider whether the rope was secured enough to bear our weight. When it was my turn to ride, I held tightly to the rope and I was pushed very high above ground. I recalled shouting loudly, *"oh, I'm in heaven!"*

Our great-uncle Malcolm, who lived quite a distance away on a hill overlooking grandma's house, heard the commotion and probably saw us airborne, too. On reflection, it was a blessing our uncle intervened, as the rope was a type of vine, tree bark, and it would have worn loose eventually. Our uncle called Mammy Darling to alert her of our dangerous escapade.

The next day, grandma asked our neighbour to cut the rope from the tree. At the time, I thought my uncle was a miserable man, but in retrospect, I am grateful. If one of us had lost our grip on the rope and fell, we would have landed in a spread of thorny rose bushes and stinging nettles. Great-uncle Malcolm (RIP) did the right thing and I am thankful he intervened because he cared for our safety, but it's fair to say our childhood innocence got our worst judgment.

We played risky games at times too and we were lucky to escape unharmed. We often used coconut palm fronds for this game. We used to sit on a frond and slide down a hill. They say ignorance is bliss, and we were oblivious to danger. Anything could have happened. Bits of broken glass or sharp pebbles could have been embedded in our legs or bottoms. I thank God we were lucky.

There was another vine, not a root plant, which reminds me of spaghetti. It grows like a leafless parasite vine. All we needed to do was break a bit of the vine, throw it on another plant and it would grow and spread rapidly.

It is called a "love vine", and there was an ole wives' saying—if you wanted to know if someone was in love with you, you could break off a bit of the love vine, throw it on another plant, and shout the person's name. If the love vine grew rapidly, your romantic relationship would blossom and have a happy outcome.

Love vine plant

Imitation Is The Sincerest Form Of Flattery

My sister Polly set the trend in fashion, and I liked to emulate her. By the time she was ten years old she had her ears pierced and often wore a pair of lovely earrings to church. I wore clip-on earrings, and by the time that I arrived at church, I had to remove my earrings because the pain was unbearable. The clip-on earrings squeezed my ears until they were sore and painful.

Grandma knew a lady in the village that pierced ears, oh yes, I was determined to have my ears done, as I thought the pain would only last a short time. My grandma agreed to let me have my ears pierced and arranged a time for me to go to the lady's home to have it done. I went alone to have my ears pierced and it was extremely painful.

When I entered her home, I noticed a little platter that contained soft grease, a wooden bottle cork, and a needle and thread on a small table. To begin, the lady rubbed a little soft grease (not even anaesthetic) on both ears, and then placed the bottle cork directly behind the spot on my ear. She pierced the flesh and pulled the thread right through then she repeated the process on the other ear. It was amazing the courage and bravery it took for me to complete the second ear.

As I left her home I thought at the time, "mission accomplished", but the healing process was prolonged, as my pierced ears turned septic. Every morning, Grandma needed to wash the wounds with disinfectant, turn the thread, and wiped it clean. Imagine having a piece of thread through a wound with dried scabs and having to pull the thread to clean it. It was excruciating, but I knew if I were patient, it would get better, and it did. The wounds healed, and my grandma bought me some lovely gold earrings.

Finally, my ear piercing was a success. But I was one of the luckier girls in the neighbourhood. Some girls who had their ears pierced using that method developed ear infections that caused the flesh to grow (they called this disfigurement "nooko"). The nooko flesh grew and hung like earrings, a terrible price to pay for costume fashion. Those unlucky girls were disfigured for life.

One day, I was walking home from school with my sister and some friends. A man lived at New Grounds village that was said to resemble a barn owl without feathers. People teased him and made squeaky noises like an owl whenever they saw him. The "ugly man" carried a cutlass in his hand, in a way, to dissuade people from provoking him, and I suspect for his own protection. When I saw him coming towards us, I was quick on the mark to play a practical joke.

I was always the mischievous one looking for trouble, and I began to laugh. I cleverly included a squeaky noise, like an owl. My sister knew exactly why I was laughing that way, and she said, "*oh, Gar . . . 'e go chop yo*". (*oh, God . . . he would chop you.*) I was lucky, though. He didn't acknowledge the bantering and walked by quietly.

Aunt Cynthia played a practical joke on me as I sat on our neighbour mother Welch's front doorsteps late one evening. My aunt called for me to come home, and on my way to the house, it was about fifty yards away, I heard strange groans, so I looked to my right and saw an image, like a ghost in the dark. I literally flew into the house and ran up four concrete steps. Mammy Darling was sitting in her favourite rocking chair, listening to the radio. I leapt onto her lap, trembling like a leaf, hugged her, and laid my head between her comforting breasts. I remember grandma always smelt of lifebuoy soap. I was still shocked and pretrified but the joke was on me. By that time, my auntie had revealed my horror she had covered herself from head to toe with a white sheet. When I saw the image I thought it was a ghost and my immediate reaction was to run for my life.

We had a bull dog named Doso, and he often had bitches visited him in the yard. One day, we were busy playing relay race, and I ran around the kitchen building and noticed Doso was stuck to the other dog. I ran in a panic to grandma and said, "*oh, lard . . . Doso stick on e kar move*". (*Doso and the other dog are stuck together*).

"Sweet child"; came Mammy Darling reply. She didn't explain, but she fetched her broom and separated Doso from what I know now was his compromising position. Childhood innocence can create some of the best comedies.

Some of the timber houses sat on long posts like stilts, so children often played underneath the houses in the basement. One day, my younger cousins Fred and Sinclair were playing, and our auntie was in labour delivering her baby in the bedroom above the basement. When the baby cried, Sinclair stopped, turned to Fred, and said, "*listen me hay wan cat a barl*". (listen *I heard a cat meowing*). Sinclair didn't realise he was referring to Auntie's newborn son Colin entering the World. I was about ten years old. Fred and Sinclair were just a few years younger, and I thought it was classic comedy.

I have done some wild and barbaric things, especially to insects and creepy crawlies, even after my great-grandma told me they were God's creatures. Butterflies were my main target, and I would catch a butterfly, shove a bit of stick up the butterflies bum, and let it fly. At the time, I thought it was hilarious. We used to catch lizards and cut their tails off. I did it for fun, but I know it was cruel. May the good Lord forgive me!

Polly and I were privileged to have some board games, such as ludo and snakes and ladders to play with, and we often played these games with Mammy Darling. She won every time, and I'm sure she cheated because whenever she won us, she would laugh uncontrollably.

My first books at school were tales of *Mr. Joe Builds a House*. I adored the stories of Brer Anancy and Miss Tibbs. We also had a few storybooks at home, and one of the first books I read was the *Three Little Pigs*. At the time, it was one of my favourite books. My favourite story of all was *Cinderella*. Polly and I often sat quietly reading it.

I adored the pictures and the happy ending. *Red Riding Hood* scared me, but at the same time, it was fascinating. *Hansel and Gretel* was another amazing book that captivated my little mind. We also read about Robin Hood and his Merry Men. I remember a school play in which my cousin Dandy was dressed up in a Robin Hood costume.

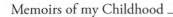

My grandparents kept encyclopedias, and my sister and I spent many happy hours looking through them pictures of dinosaurs, different kinds of cats, birds, horses, dogs, and fish. We learned at a very young age that the encyclopedia was a convenient way to learn about Mother Nature.

Treat Everyone With Kindness

Whenever someone passed away in the village, it was common for the old folks to tell us children that if we stayed out after dark, the person who had just passed away would appear in front of us as a ghost. I learned to be afraid of the dark at an early age. With the exception of my grandparents, who were conscious of our vulnerability, other grown-up people were not very tactful. They were not aware of the fact that scaremongering could have a negative effect on children. I often lay in bed at night thinking of a scary ghost manifesting itself in the dark bedroom

Gran often said; *"You mustn't be afraid of ghosts, but be afraid of the living, as there are plenty more scary things around us"*. However, that was no comfort to me.

In the village where I lived, boys learned to swim by the time they were in their early teens. The swimming pool was a part of the river in which they'd dug a deep hole. They removed the stones and soil, and it made a perfect swimming pool. On weekends and school holidays, the boys would get together down by the riverside, where they learned to swim and dive.

Girls weren't allowed to go roaming without an aunt or a grandmother. The old folks believed it would stop teenage girls from meeting boys and winding up with an unwanted pregnancy, but it wasn't one hundred percent foolproof. Some girls did fall pregnant, but it probably minimised the birth rates for teenage girls by parents being strict and protective.

One day, I was playing hide and seek with my cousins and sister. Banana trees grow as single plant or several plants bunched together, so I went to hide between the banana trees and sat behind the huge trunks. I sat quietly for a few minutes, but by that time, I was covered in red ants. One bit me in my eye, and I was in agony. My sister and cousins didn't need to search for me as I ran screaming. Grandma assisted me. She decided the only way to alleviate the pain was to spray breast milk into my eye. Grandma and I went to a neighbour, and she sprayed her breast milk in my eye. It's amazing how effective traditional medicines work as the pain improved very quickly.

I went to the village shop for grandma frequently. One day, I was standing in the shop, and the shopkeeper was serving a tall man from another village. I was just tall enough to reach the shop counter, and I placed five dollars on the high counter, but when it was time for me to pay the shopkeeper for the groceries I had bought, the money and the man had vanished. He stole my money. Later years, that man committed suicide. Apparently, he went to the beach, walked into the sea, and kept walking.

Do Not Take Life Too Seriously; No One Gets Out Alive

My family taught me a few superstitions, and they remain at the forefront of my mind:

> If I was going somewhere, and I needed to go back because I'd forgotten something, my grandmothers would shout, *"turn back a bad luck!"* They believed that if you set out on a journey and then turned back it brought you bad luck.

> If I got dressed and accidently put a garment on inside out, my grandmothers told me that it was good luck to reverse the garment at noon, but I was always rebellious and ignored that rule.

> My grandmothers also told me that when I was chatting with someone if by chance I were to forget what I was about to say, I should scratch my head—then I would remember what I was about to say. Not always true!

> My mother told me in her days when a woman gave birth it was custom for the mother to stay in bed for nine days. During convalescent period the house was often in darkness curtains closed in day light. The reason for this they believed the baby that came from a dark womb should be gradually introduced into day light. When they cleaned the house the rubbish was swept up in a pile in one corner for nine days until that period ended.

Sometimes at night, an owl flew by and made a noisy squeak. The old folks would shout, *"go to another area"*. The old folks believed when an owl flew by with noisy squeak at night it was a bad omen, a premonition of death.

It Is Better To Light A Candle Than To Curse The Darkness

When the moon shone, we sat on the doorsteps, and I loved to watch the night sky. It was clear blue and laden with hundreds of stars. I saw some of the stars jumped from one spot to another. My aunt told me that the jumping stars were satellites. While we observed the night sky, my family told me that babies came from airplanes. I guess my family thought it was too complicated to explain to me about the "birds and bees."

When night falls in St Vincent, insect noises fill the air. It is not an annoying sound, but natural wildlife in sync with the darkness. It is serene. When I was growing up, insect noises produced tranquil background sounds in different melodies, and listening to them was a good way to relax, unwind, and de-stress the mind prior to bedtime.

At night, the darkness set the perfect scene for me to be afraid. My imagination went wild, and the ghosts lurking outside seemed real. Whenever we travelled at night, it was normally several of us. I would position myself to walk in the middle so I wasn't the last person because I often imagined something spooky was following us. A banana leaf swaying in the wind at night (especially on moonlit nights) was enough to set my heart racing.

Moonlit nights created perfectly scary images outside, and Gran would say, "*cowards die many times before their deaths*". Besides, this happened after I listened to scary tales from big people who should have known better. However, it's not all bad. I'd learned an important lesson—always be cautious with children and don't tell them silly fantasies that can cause jitters.

I enjoyed sing-alongs with the family in the evenings, especially when the moon was shining. On those nights, it was a perfect setting for families and neighbours to sit outdoors and enjoy the night before bedtime on the weekends. The old folks played card games while the children played skipping rope game, and the ladies prepared many snacks, such as roast corn or roasted breadnuts. It was like a barbecue, but with the accompanying nighttime background noises of insects. Every year, there was a new dance craze, just like an annual fashion parade and we used to practice the new dance rhythms.

An insect called a "larbell" flew around in the dark—a blinking beetle-like creature with its own torch. We saw small twinkling lights in the air every evening. Now I know they are commonly called fireflies. One night, I was curious to find out if the larbell's light still shined the next morning, so I caught a larbell and kept it under a glass overnight. The next morning, all was revealed, and the light still shone from the larbell's posterior.

One time, I visited a hospital for the elderly at Glen. It was an unforgettable experience. I saw an old lady without a nose, just a big hole in her face where her nose used to be. I still remembered her words as clear as a bell. She was shouting, "*gimme the piece of bread let me drink the cup of tea*". I was traumatised by her disfigurement. I wonder if my grandmother had realised the impact it had on me. I couldn't explain how it made me feel at the time but it was an incredible moment of despair.

Union Is Strength

Many ladies who learned the art of handicraft designs manufactured handbags, baskets, and tablemats using the leaves from a plant called "copeo." To begin the process, they collected the leaves in big containers. It took several days to alter the leaves before they could start moulding them into shape. First, to make the leaves strong and flexible, they boiled them to extract the photosynthesis. After boiling the leaves, they spread them out to dry in the hot sun.

The next step was to alter the sun-dried leaves. They used a big knife to straighten the leaves by holding the leaf firmly and pulling the knife across the long leaf. This was an easy task, and children used to help their mothers and aunts. This technique made the leaves more flexible for weaving. For a sturdy basket or handbag, they used bits of green sticks from coconut fronds.

Finally, after processing the leaves, the women sat for hours working on ladies' handbags and shopping baskets. It was hard work, but therapeutic, as the women sat in a communal area chatting and listening to the radio as they worked. While they worked, they watched the children play nearby. They made handbags of all sizes and shapes and finished off the handbags and baskets with clever embroidery designs. The handbags were sold to local traders and exported all over the Caribbean, UK, America, and Canada.

The calabash capsules grow from a sturdy tree and looks like a big, round, green fruit (but I call it a pod), and when the calabash pods are fully grown, they are the size of a watermelon. Most farmers used calabash capsules as crockery and to store water while they work the land. To make a calabash into bowls, the pod is sliced into two halves and the inedible fleshy bits inside the outer shell are removed from the pod. When the flesh is removed from the calabash pod, the hollow shell is left to dry. The dried calabash bowl hardens and turns brown, almost like pottery, and people used the calabash bowls as crockery and to store water.

The local tinsmith in our village was very inventive. He made cups and pots out of tin cans and sold them to villagers to use as kitchen utensils. The cups and pots were most suitable for outdoor cooking, and farm workers used them to cook meals when they were working in the fields.

As soon as girls became teenagers, they attended sewing classes to learn dressmaking or handicrafts. Normally, the teacher was a seamstress or a lady from the village with handicraft skills. They held small dressmaking classes in their homes to teach teenage girls, and as payment, the pupils took care of the laundry or ironing. Some seamstresses earned income, sewing dresses for local people. The fabric to make clothes was sold at the tiny village shops. Men who did tailoring for a living ran apprentice classes for teenage boys.

Most women had some of their dresses made by a local seamstress. The women would purchase fabric, thread, and zipper then chose a style from a fashion catologue. The seamstress created exact replicas of dresses from the fashion catalogue and she charged a small fee for the finished product. It was exciting to collect a dress that was designed exactly like my sister's, as we frequently wore the same style of dress, and people often thought we were twins.

There were other classes available for women to learn embroidery, tapestry, and crochet. Church groups organized these classes. We had no registered charities in those days, so the poorest people relied on neighbours giving away their old clothes, but there was a stigma attached, as Vincies called charity handouts *"thank-u-marm,"* and they didn't hesitate to point out someone wearing hand-me-down charity clothes it was obvious prejudice during that time.

It was normal to see men and boys wearing their trousers with a piece of string instead of a belt, and young boys from poor families usually had huge holes or patchwork on their pants. Some people couldn't afford to buy clothes for their children to go to school, and those children stayed home to help their parents provide the next meal.

Earthquakes

As I recollect, natural disaster such earthquakes often occurred at night and I was lucky I slept through them, but the next morning at school, everyone talked about how scared they were when they were woken by an earthquake. One night during an earthquake, the whole house shook and my sister tried to wake me, but Gran told her not to scare me. The next morning, I felt very lucky to have escaped the fright.

Mammy Darling had a cabinet she called her wagon, which kept her wares on display in the sitting room. She often told us that the cups were her best china for when she had visitors. One day, there was an earthquake it was the first time I'd witness one, and I thought the World was ending. When the cabinet shook, I thought all of grandma's wares would break so grandma held onto the cabinet to stop her wares from breaking. It was a short earthquake and lasted only seconds. I remember thinking if that was a light tremor I dreaded a strong one. This experience was a lesson for me and I think natural disasters helped me believe God does exist.

Hurricane

During hurricane season, it rained heavily for hours, sometimes all day. Thunderstorms were not dangerous back then, and we often sheltered under a big branchy tree. Whenever grandma and I were caught out in a heavy rainstorm, she would pick a big tania or dasheen leaf for me to use as an umbrella. The raindrops just formed little balls on the leaf, as it was almost waterproof and didn't rip or leak.

In rainstorms, we heard strong winds howling through the banana plantations. Through the window, I could see the tall coconut trees swung low, as though they would break into pieces, and some did. It was very scary during stormy weather. In heavy rainfall, rivers overflowed, and people who lived across the rivers without bridges got stranded. They couldn't go home and had to seek shelter, sometimes overnight, with family or friends. Dead animals and hundreds of coconuts and other debris floated in the heavy floodwaters, travelling at speed down the river.

Hurricane season is from June to November, but it is stormy from September to November in St Vincent. I remember the heavy rainfall caused landslides, and many tarmac roads were blocked with fallen trees. After a storm, many banana plantations were destroyed. I saw fields of fallen banana trees everywhere I looked. Many crops such vegetables destroyed by the floods, and the farmers had to re-plant the fallen banana trees. They did this by slicing off the top of the fallen trees and planting the rooted end. The trees quickly sprouted again in the warm sunshine.

The low valley area where we lived made it a scary place during stormy weather. A big coconut tree in our neighbour's garden hung dangerously over our house. When the clouds turned grey and dark and strong gales blew, I often felt nervous of the fact that several tall trees were close to the house, but the coconut tree was the most threatening. It was frightening to watch the neighbour's coconut tree sway in gale forced winds. The coconut tree had a long thin trunk and when the strong winds blew it moved the tree backwards and forwards very low almost to breaking point directly over our home, but it managed to stay intact.

Dreams Can Come True When Imagination Meets Reality

I climbed the La Soufriere mountain at age eleven to see the volcano. Prior to the trip, my aunt prepared plenty of food. I was very excited and looked forward to the expedition with my sister and friends. We set off early by bus to Georgetown about six miles from home, and as we approached Dry River, the area leading to La Soufriere mountain, I knew it was a sensational place.

At Dry River, where a big wide river once flowed to the sea, I saw the derelict remains black sand and scattering of big stones. In those days, the road was narrow and rugged so we had to make our way by foot to climb up the La Soufriere mountain. We began the strenuous trek up the steep terrain to see the volcano. As the saying goes, ignorance is bliss, and I was very excited on that bright, sunny morning. Some people carried bottled drinks and a walking stick to help them climb the steep mountain. My aunt stayed at the riverbed with our lunch in a big wicker basket. There were groups of people from all over the island, so the atmosphere was lively.

We set off my—sister, cousins, and other friends from school. Everton kept repeating an advert that was broadcasting over the radio at the time. It was "*Vicks for colds and for coughs*", and we interpreted it as "vicks for colds and f . . . offs".

It was my first big challenge climbing the La Soufriere mountain, and the climb seemed like it went on forever and ever. The more hills I climbed, the higher and more strenuous it was. As we approached the volcano, the hilltop was misty and covered in thick clouds, and at first glance, it seemed as though the sky and ground were conjoined.

I remember the temperature felt very cold, as if the mist was raining droplets of ice, similar to foggy conditions in the UK. At the summit, the volcano looked like a large lake stretching deep down between the rocks, and the water was almost emerald green. Some people threw small pebbles, but the stones didn't land in the water.

A big lake of green water that is in fact like a bubbling pot. I can only describe my first sight of the volcano as phenomenal and eerie. On the island of St Vincent the La Soufriere is like a time bomb, and I've read that volcanoes are fickle. La Soufriere, even dormant, is like a sleeping giant waiting to erupt. The next day, my entire body was sore from climbing the steep mountain.

Great Grandma Malady told me about the time La Soufriere erupted in 1902. The next morning, when they tried to open their front doors, the ash from the volcano was so thick they were barricaded in their homes. I remember one day people believed the volcano was about to burst, and the entire island went very dark. There were heavy clouds travelling at speed and there was a sense of panic around the village. I remember thinking we were all going to die, but after some hours had passed, it gradually became calm and bright again.

The most recent volcanic eruption in St Vincent was in 1979. It was the same year Mum booked a holiday to St Vincent from England. The day before she travelled, we heard that the volcano was belching out ashes. Mum continued her journey to St Vincent, even though we were concerned for her safety. She told us she would go with God's blessings.

Mum often recalled how scary it was, especially when she arrived from London at Barbados airport. Everyone kept telling her she shouldn't travel to St Vincent. However, she continued, and when she arrived at Arnos Vale Airport, it was gloomy, as there was volcano dust everywhere. A few days after Mum arrived in St Vincent, everything went calm again. The volcano eruption had ended. La Soufriere's ashes can reach as far away as Barbados, which is one hundred and nine miles from St Vincent.

The La Soufriere volcano is no longer a lake with emerald green water. Since it erupted in 1979, it has formed a rock in the middle of the crater. Only scientists can determine whether it is still active. I know what I would prefer it to be. I've learned that volcanoes can lay dormant for hundreds of years and suddenly erupt. A volcano occurs when magma (hot molten rock) is expelled through an opening in the earth's crust.

The melting of the earth's interior forms magma and molten rock is lighter than solid rock. It floats, so the magma rises. The reason the volcano erupts depends on what happens to the rising magma. It may cool and crystallise to form new rock, but it may also break through to erupt. Scientists believe it is very difficult to predict when a volcano will erupt, but they understand what makes volcanoes awaken.

Springtime—Mango Season

The seasonal changes in St Vincent are not as obvious as the seasonal changes in England because the temperature is constantly warm. However, in St Vincent, we distinguished the seasons according to the crops harvested. For instance, when the mango trees were laden with blossoms and the birds sang more melodies, it was springtime, but we called it "mango season." At a very young age, my sister, cousins, and I interpreted one of the melodies the birds sang. It was "*Uncle Eric mango a ripe*". Crazy, I know, but it was lucid to us our unique intrepretion.

As the temperature cooled at night, ripe mangoes fell from the trees, and we woke early to collect the mangoes even from our neighbour's gardens. There are three flavours of mango—fleshy, sweet and juicy, or stringy—hairy type of mangoes so we often walked to the gardens with the sweet juicy mango trees, actually stealing them, but it wasn't a big problem. There are several variety of mangoes grown in St Vincent; some grow in bunches, and others grow as single fruit.

The mangoes have names, too, and I used to think rich people owned most of the good quality sweet mangoes. Some mangoes when they are ripe turn red or yellow and some stay green, and our family had a fleshy type and a few sweet and juicy mango trees in our garden.

Some mangoes mature at a tiny size, which we called "bubby suck mango." They are tiny and shaped like breast and nipple, hence the name, and they are just as the fully-grown mangoes, ripe and juicy to eat. Most mango trees have huge trunks, so it is virtually impossible to climb into some of the bigger mango trees, as the trunks are too large.

So we used to collect small stones and try to hit the ripe mangoes hanging in the tree. Sometimes we hit the ripe mangoes, and other times we hit the mangoes that were too young to eat.

Some fruit were seasonal; for instance, mangoes might be in season from May to August. We had a mammee apple tree in our garden, this was uncommon, as only a few people had a mammee tree in their garden. The mammee apple grows on a tall sturdy tree and the fruit is similar in colour to a pumpkin. It has bright orange flesh on a stone and when ripe it is ready to eat straight from the tree. A fully-grown mammee apple is the size of a watermelon and the skin is dark brown and almost leathery in texture. The taste is similar to a cantaloupe.

We ate a variety of homegrown tropical fruits—golden apples, hog plums, plum roses, guavas, custard apples, sugar apples, bell apples, soursops, oranges, tangerines, and several flavours of mangoes. If any of the fruits were not in our family's garden, and it was ok, we picked a few from the gardens of our friendly neighbours.

What is greater than the mind, the poor have it,
the rich don't need it, and if you don't feed it, you'll die.

Answer: ***HUNGER***

Don't Fear Pressure For Pressure Is What Turns
Rough Stones Into Diamonds

Banana Shipment

When I was about five years old, I remember men who worked for the Banana Association sprayed the Island's tall banana trees in the fields with pesticides regularly. The workers carried a big metal box filled with pesticides strapped to their back. The container had a nozzle that the men pulled to spray the bananas leaves. It was a scary time for young children. I was petrified of the men carrying the green, noisy machines. I thought they looked like aliens, and when they were spraying the bananas leaves in our garden, I hid indoors. Children were well behaved until the men who sprayed the banana leaves had left the garden.

I vividly recall a time when Mammy Darling's helper was ill. My cousin Melanie and I were reluctant assistants. We had to carry a bunch of bananas on our head and we travelled a narrow dirt track to where the banana truck was parked by the main road. Melanie was very young—eight years old at the time—and the bunch of bananas were very heavy. As she struggled up the hill, she began to curse aloud. She said; "*Me na know wey dem gimme dis f . . . ing heavy banana to carry*". I couldn't stop laughing, even though I was under pressure, too. It was unusual to hear someone as young as my cousin using rude language, so it was quite comical at the time.

The easy way to carry a bunch of bananas, we used a katta on our head to ease the weight. There are two types of kattas—one that is made from dried leaves, and one that is made from cloth. First, you shape the material into a thick, long string. Then you roll the long string in a circle and fasten the loose end into part of the circle.

When You Tell The Truth,
You Don't Have To Remember Anything

The katta is shaped like a round cushion with a hole in the middle, and it was used to seat the heavy load such as a bunch of bananas or a basket of freshly dug up heavy vegetables from the farmland. The katta lessened the pressure from the heavy load, and I think the hole in the middle of the katta seated the heavy load securely. Hence the reason why I often saw people walking with heavy load balanced on their head. Children used to help their parents when it was banana shipment day they carried a brunch of bananas balanced on the head to the banana depot for inspection, and some men even carried two bunches of bananas piled them high one on top the other.

The banana association authority in St Vincent needed to uphold certain standards regarding the quality of bananas that the UK authority would allow for import trade. Obviously, some bananas were rejected during inspection, and growers relied on the revenue from the sale of bananas as it was their livelihood. So, it used to cause enormous hardship if bananas were rejected they got no sale.

I recall one day at New Grounds banana association depot there was a fatal accident. One of the supervisors kept a sharp knife in his shirt pocket and the knife pierced his chest, but he kept working until someone saw blood on his shirt. He bled to death, as in those days, there was no emergency ambulance service available. The untimely death of a young health man affected the entire community.

Farmers grew various types of bananas in St Vincent, and different islands in the Caribbean have different names for them.

Unlike the fig, lackatan, and gramashell, which are edible when ripe, the plantain is only edible when it is cooked, roasted, or fried. The mafobay (spelt maugh faugh baugh) is only edible when it is cooked or roasted. The green plantain is used to make savoury dish. Unripe plantains are peeled, thinly sliced, and deep-fried to make plantain crisp, and ripe plantains are sliced thinly and fried to make a side dish.

The flesh of a green banana or plantain is covered by a hard skin which contains a sticky gluey liquid, and I recall our grandmothers often told us to avoid the liquid staining our hands and clothes. A green banana or plantain skin has a thick rubbery texture difficult to remove. Grandma told us the easy way to peel them, first make a deep cut about the thickness of the skin and draw the cut from the stem to tail end. That piercing makes it easier to pull away the skin from the flesh. After piercing the fruit we used to peel them while they were immersed in water or we covered our hands in cooking oil to avoid the gluey stains. I often saw farm workers wearing old clothes covered in permanent banana stains.

Banana plant

Eat Well, Stay Fit

Recipes

Gran made many delicious coconut tarts using the same ingredients for her bread recipe:

> Strong plain flour. Yeast, Margarine, Nutmeg
> Sugar, Grated coconut, Milk

You need half-a-pint of water in a saucepan bring it to boil, and then add one grated coconut or pre-packed desiccated coconut. Add a cup of brown or white sugar and let it boil until the sugar starts to caramelise. Turn the heat off and let it cool until the bread dough mixture is ready (increase). Cut the bread dough into small pieces to make the tarts.

On a floured board, roll each piece of dough one at a time into circles, adding about a tablespoon of the coconut mixture. Fold the dough with the mixture and squeeze the ends of the folded circle to seal the coconut mixture in. Put them out on greased tray and leave coconut tarts for an hour to increase in size (rise). Bake for thirty minutes using the oven temperature for baking bread. The final bit of baking instruction is optional if you like the coconut tarts sweet and sticky. You could glaze the coconut tarts with sugar and milk.

For the glaze mixture, use fifty ml of milk and three tablespoons of sugar, bring to boil, and bush the tarts with the liquid as soon as you remove them from the oven. Gran made many fried dumplings (bakes) with whatever mixture she had available at the time. We had various flavours of dumplings—ma-dung-o (cassava flour), coconut dumplings, cornmeal dumplings, dumplings with eggs, or just a tablespoon full of sugar added to the dumpling mixture. Ma-dung-o is the freshly grated starchy flour extracted from the arrowroot vegetable.

One day, my cousin crept into the kitchen. Grandma was busy frying some dumplings. My cousin was only seven years old. She stole a few of the fried bakes and hid them under her hat on her head. We looked on laughing, but Grandma was too witty; she knew exactly what was going on.

In those days, only the local shops owned fridges. Gran often requested a few ounces of butter or margarine. All perishable foods like butter and margarine had to be bought from the local shop daily. It had to be a quick dash to the shop and back. I couldn't idle on my way back with a friend or the butter would melt. Gran had somewhere cool in the kitchen where she kept the butter. Our grandmothers were excellent cooks. Every meal was freshly cooked.

I have no recorded recipes of the homemade cakes grandma baked, but I remember Mammy Darling made do-ku-na—grated sweet potatoes, grated coconut, milk, flour, spices, and sugar. Back in those days, they didn't have foil or cooking bags, so Mammy Darling used banana leaves and steamed the leaves over the flames. It made the leaf stronger and flexible, and I think the heat cleaned the pesticide from the leaves.

After she mixed the do-ku-na ingredients, she cut the banana leaves into squares, added about three tablespoons of mixture to the squared leaves, then folded the leaves like a little packet, and tied it with string. Grandma boiled the packets for at least an hour, or until the do-ku-nas were cooked. The cooked do-ku-nas looked like black clay. This happens when you mix starch and sugar together, and bring it to a boil. It turns black. The same ingredients are used to make sweet potato pudding only the mixture is baked, rather than cooked.

My grandmothers made delicious confectionaries using coconuts or peanuts. They made something they called coconut sugar cakes using a dried coconut. First, she diced the coconut into small pieces then she boiled the diced pieces until they were cooked. For the other coconut sweets, Gran grated the coconut, put it through a strainer or sieve, and then poured water over the grated coconut to squeeze out the coconut milk. After squeezing out the coconut milk, she boiled the coconut flakes with sugar and a little pink food colouring and let the mixture boil until the sugar caramelised.

As the coconut mixture thickened, she dropped several spoonfuls onto a damp tray and let it set. Grandma also used the coconut milk to make fudges. She poured the coconut milk into a saucepan, added brown sugar, and a dab of butter. While the coconut milk mixture boiled, she constantly stirred it until the sugar caramelised. She then poured the thick mixture onto a damp tray and let it cool before cutting the hardened fudge into small pieces. Grandma told me the added butter to the mixture made the fudge soft, and that without butter the fudge was hard and sticky.

The peanut sugar cakes were cooked the same way as the coconut cakes. After grandma shelled the peanuts, she baked them on hot heat in a metal pot. When they were parched, the peanuts looked golden brown. She poured them in boiling water, added brown sugar, a little root ginger, let it boil until the sugar caramelized, and then she dropped several tablespoon heaps onto a damp tray and let it set.

Tri-tri Cakes

Sometimes at night, when the clouds formed special patterns, the old folk believed it was symbolic of bountiful seafood, especially the little tiny fish they called tri-tri. When the fish was mixed to a floury paste and marinated with chopped chives and hot peppers and fried into bite-sized fritters, they made a delicious side dish we called tri-tri cakes.

Dancing Is Music Of The Soul

Every evening while grandma prepared dinner, she often listened to the radio. We received excellent broadcast coverage from Trinidad and Barbados. Grandma always listened to the program *Rolling Home*. It played a selection of calypso and music from the UK and America, so I knew about the Beatles and Elvis Presley.

One of my favourite Beatles songs is "All You Need Is Love." It remains in my heart as one of my first love songs. We also listened to Otis Redding, Jim Reeves, and Percy Sledge. "When a Man Loves a Woman" and "I've Got Dreams to Remember"; and "Cover Me" by Percy Sledge are some of my favourite love songs. Also, the song "I'm a Single Girl" by Connie Francis opened up a new chapter when I began to learn about falling in love. Vic Brooster was one of my favourite presenters on radio Barbados. He played a popular tune called "The Liquidator," and even after all these years, it is still an amazing melody. Vic Brooster always ended his program with the catch phrase "I have things to do, places to go, and people to see".

My favourite newsreaders were Victor Fernando and Marva Manning. I adored their eloquent voices and remember Marva announcing, *"Here is the seven o'clock news read by Marva Manning"*. She was one of my role models, and I often wished to be able to read the news like Marva Manning.

Grandma's radio looked like a big square metal box, and the battery to operate the radio was just as big. When the battery ran low, grandma left it outside in the hot sun for a few hours to recharge.

It worked a treat as the radio came "alive again," as grandma used to say. From time to time, she needed to unscrew the back cover of the radio to remove tiny insects that had crawled into the radio vent to avoid damage to our entertainment.

Mammy Darling had a gramophone. It was a big mahogany wood cabinet with two compartments. The top shelf housed a turntable with a lid, and on the lower shelf, grandma kept some vinyl records. At the side of the cabinet, there was a gadget to fit a removable handle, which was used to rotate the turntable that played the records. The volume key was at the front of the cabinet. One of the songs grandma used to play was, *"Matilda, Yo Tek me Money and Garn Venezuela"*.

The gramophone is now where most old appliances in St Vincent have gone, as people are notorious for destroying heirlooms, but in our culture, it is common to hear people say, "*me na warnt dead leff,*" (I don't want the belongings of a deceased person) and they destroy most old appliances left by dead relatives.

One of our neighbours in the village composed a song about her husband and grandson. The title of the song was "*Curry Buck garn a Trinidad*". It was easy, catchy, and had rude lyrics to learn. One day, I started singing the song, and my grandmother wasn't too pleased, but Gran was always conscious that we follow her high standards, and she was against us emulating neighbours who she believed had no scruples.

There was gossip in the village regarding the husband that our neighbour composed the song about. Apparently, he had a sick toe, and it wouldn't heal, so he took drastic action and used a sharp razor to slice the toe off.

To this day, I cannot confirm whether this was true or false, but I believe he was the type of person who would be strong and brave enough to take such action.

Sometimes my sister and friends walked to high grass lands near our homes. We found a place where the fatpork plum grew wild. When ripe, they turned red. The flesh was white and sweet, like coconut jelly, and if I ate too many, they gave me indigestion. Grandma warned us not to eat too many of the plums, but I couldn't resist, and I often felt bloated after trips to the fatpork field. When we returned home and grandma asked us how far we'd walked, we couldn't lie, as the bud grass on our clothes was a giveaway. Bud grass attached to clothes when we walked in overgrown bushes. They were very difficult to remove. Our clothes were hand washed, so they wanted us to remove the bud grass prior to laundry day.

Fatpork plant

Mysteries

To Get Out Of Difficulty, One Usually Must Go Through It

One night, I was following my cousins to the shop, which was a ten-minute walk from home. It was about six p.m., and already dark, so we carried a torch. We had to walk through a deep valley surrounded by high hills, and as we approached an area called Marie Hole, stretching as far as the eyes could see there was a field of wild lilies. As we approached the field of wild lilies, we saw something race up the hill, and a single light. It was impossible for it to be human; it had to be a wild animal of some kind to travel up the hill through thick bushes at such speed. In the panic that took place, I collided with Marjorie, and we screamed so loud the neighbours came out to assist us.

When we told them what we saw, they told us it must have been a Jack lantern. People often talked about Jack lanterns, and everyone had the same story—they spotted something at night with a light that was not human. What is a Jack lantern? Does such a thing exist? Some people believe a Jack lantern is a nocturnal animal with a light attached to its head. What we saw that night was certainly an animal with a light. Where does it live in the daytime and how big is it? I know it is very quick on its feet.

The night scene from my grandparents' home overlooking the villages of Lowman's Windward, Gregg's, and Maroon Hill was a mystery to Polly and me. When darkness fell, we could see single lights, especially at Maroon Hill, and the light would move quickly and then disappear—clearly, an island mystery!

Uncle Jack visited our home frequently and often stayed after dark chatting and joking; as a rule, he left quietly without saying good night. Apparently, he left quietly because he believed if he said good night, ghosts would follow him home. Uncle Jack had to walk a rugged

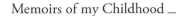

footpath through banana and coconut plantations then cross a river and climb a stony hill in total darkness with just a flashlight to guide him safely home.

An old lady in the village believed she was clairvoyant and often interpreted her bad dreams as premonitions. After a bad dream that night she came out early morning and carried a bell. She rang the bell and shouted; "*The river was muddy; sudden death, oh!*" The noise of the ringing bell woke me up and I remembered thinking that message was spooky and terrifying to hear first thing in the morning. For the rest of the day, I waited to hear bad news, but luckily, her predictions didn't produce any results.

The Pursuit Of Happiness Is The Chase Of A Lifetime

Migration— "Everybody garn a England"!

By the time I was eight years old, nearly all of my aunts, uncles, mum and dad had migrated to England. My sister Polly, my cousins, and I were left with our grandparents to care for us, so we made up a song comprising the names of family members who were in England. We often sang the melody, naming each family member. This was an enormous boon to the healing process from feeling abandoned. Still all was not lost, as we enjoyed many lovely gifts sent to us from abroad.

The local post office was just across the road from our primary school in New Grounds. Every day, people gathered at the post office at a certain time in the morning to listen to Mrs. Robinson yell the roll call of addressees who received letters and parcels from America, Canada, or the UK.

Mammy Darling received registered letters enclosed with cheques, and it was a joy to read letters from relatives in England. It meant also that I would accompany grandma to shop in Kingstown, and I looked forward to the trip enthusiastically. My grandparents received parcels from England regularly. It was always exciting, as the parcels contained many goodies.

When grandma collected the parcel from the post office, we used to gather around, especially if it was from Mum as Polly and I received most of the items. I had a leather book bag and a long, pink, hooded raincoat. I felt very special in my plastic raincoat, which kept my school uniform dry when it rained heavily.

The postmistress's family had a bakery, too, and they made various cakes to sell. By mid-day, the delicious aroma had drifted across the schoolyard. They sold mauby and cakes at lunchtime to school children. The mauby drink is a traditional drink in some Caribbean Islands. Vincentians use the bark of the mauby tree and boiled over high heat for thirty minutes, added clove, and allow the beverage liquid to cool before adding sugar to taste.

Coconut drops and coconut tarts were two my favourite cakes from the Robinson bakery. The postmistress made a roaring trade catering for school children lunch and during banana shipment days, the school and banana inspection depot was just a short distance from the Robinson's bakery and post office.

"The Girl From—'Country'..."

Mammy Darling often made plans the night before she went shopping in Kingstown, usually to travel on Saturday morning. I often felt so excited I couldn't sleep Friday night. In those days, as many as fifty percent of villagers could not afford to travel by bus to Kingstown, and neighbours used to rely on grandma to purchase small items, such as a tube of ointment, nothing bulky to weigh her down.

We woke early at six a.m. to catch the bus. Grandma and I walked to the main road, and we stood outside the local shop. This was where the bus stopped to pick up passengers. I can still remember the excitement I felt while waiting for the bus to arrive.

The bus was designed to carry passengers and their provisions to market in Kingstown. There were limited seats for adults, let alone for children, so I sat on grandma's lap. The bus carried passengers and farmers and their trading products, mainly fruits and vegetables sold in market stalls. Some people made handbags and baskets from copeo and willow plants. It was normal to see a lot of luggage tied on the roof top of buses travelling to Kingstown. On Saturdays, Kingstown harbour was busy with traders buying and selling to other islands as far south as Trinidad.

The bus made several stops en route to Kingstown. The journey took over an hour. We normally travelled by the bus Bridgetown Surprise, but all of the buses had names written just above the windscreen. This made it easy to distinguish where the bus owners came from and the destination of travel. The owner who drove Bridgetown Surprise bus was a short fat man with a gold-toothed smile.

When we arrived in Kingstown by the bus terminal, a few local residents used to shout, "*country bookie come a town*"! The country people often referred to town residents as "town rats." This regional snobbery still exists, and it is done to denigrate a person who lives outside Kingstown zone. Some Kingstown residents would not mention the regional areas in St Vincent by name. They use two words to define the island; it's "town" or "country," and "country" symbolises anywhere in St Vincent that is not within a five-mile radius of Kingstown.

From a very young age, I often went shopping in Kingstown with Mammy Darling. The lovely dress I wore looked untidy and crushed from sitting in a cramped space. As soon as we arrived in Kingstown after the long journey, I needed the bathroom. The toilet cubicle was an unpleasant experience; it was not very clean, but it was always a welcome relief.

The cheques grandma received from Mum and other family members in the England, had to be exchanged for cash at the Kingstown General Post Office. Mammy Darling realised the long wait in the post office queue would be unbearable for me, so she bought me popcorn sold in a brown paper bag with a sprinkling of salt from a shop just opposite the post office.

Grandma's postal orders needed an official signature, so she used to go to the police barracks seeking approval from one of the police inspectors she knew from New Grounds village. Inspector Bob, Jackson, and Stoddard—any of those men authorised grandma's postal orders prior to exchanging them for cash.

There was always a long queue at the post office, and people stretching out on the sidewalk. It took a while for grandma to exchange her postal orders for cash, but it was okay for me I didn't notice the long wait as I munched my popcorn.

Travelling around Kingstown was such a buzz. I loved it for the good things on sale. I felt anxious of losing my grandma in the crowd, so when she was laden with heavy bags I grabbed onto her dress so that I didn't get lost in the crowd. I thought the shops in Kingstown were massive; at the time, it was the focal point of all enterprises, dwellings, and all the good food in the supermarkets. We bought sapodillas, and an assortment of plums. I also enjoyed a special drink, a snow cone sold by men riding bicycle carts. It was my treat from grandma for the bus ride journey home. The snow cone was made from crushed ice, covered with red, fruity liquid, and garnished with evaporated milk. I think the name is appropriate as the cup looks like a cone and the crushed ice is like snow.

A man stood by the market place selling vanilla ice cream from a refrigerated cart and shouting all day long he said; "*ice cream, get your ice cream*". One day, my cousin Dandy and I, we were walking by the market place in Kingstown, and Dandy responded; "*me could scream, too*"! I remember an old lady walked around Kingstown dressed in rags, my sister and I named her Pippyre because her ragged clothes reminded us of feathers. She actually looked like a bird.

As I walked around the shops with Mammy Darling, I used to beg her to buy me everything I saw especially toys. It is only now that I realised how infuriating it must have been. Sometimes I carried my own small change in my little handbag, but the money I carried was just enough to buy an ice cream.

The Sunrise and Sardine bakery shops in Kingstown sold various cakes. If Mammy Darling went in one bakery and her favourite cakes were sold out, she went to the other bakery. If Grandma failed to find her cakes in Kingstown, she would wait until we were travelling back home. The bus often stopped at the next bakery at Arnos Vale, where passengers purchased cakes.

The bakery also sold bread Vincentians called "machine bread," simply because the dough was mixed using a bread machine. The shops closed at four p.m., and all buses rolled out of Kingstown, as it was safer to arrive at their destinations before it darkness fell, as during that time, there were no streetlights, so drivers had to rely on the floodlights from vehicles.

There were two bus terminals in Kingstown—one for the windward area, located outside the court house—the other for the leeward buses opposite the market area. The market traders often gathered around the bus terminals, seeking last minute trades. The vendors were mainly women selling sweets, peanuts, peanut cakes, coconut sugar cakes, ginger sticks, journeyman, popcorn in paper bags, plums, and mangoes, and men on bicycle carts selling ice cream and snow cones. The journeyman was made from grated coconut caramelised with molasses and boiled into toffee fudge. It's an appropriate name as it really kept me quiet on the journey home, munching away my sticky journeyman fudge.

The "iron man" statue springs to mind as one of the distinctive landmarks in Kingstown. The iron man used to face the courthouse in Kingstown but today it is standing in a different spot looking towards the sea. As we approached Kingstown, the juice drinks factory was another popular landmark. I saw juice bottle drinks filling up on the assembly lines as we drove by the factory. The two big stores Edward D. Lane and United Traders; both are still in business today. Edward D. Lane's first floor housed several cabinets with glass windows and glass tops. At the time, I was just tall enough to peep through the glass window displays at the jewellery glittering under the lights. Grandma

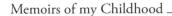

used to say, "*all that glitters is not gold*", as the cosmetic jewellery on display were cheap gold plated ones.

One year, around Christmastime, a passenger boat travelling from Bequia to Kingstown capsized, killing everyone on board. The principal of the Girls' High school was on board; and it plunged the school into mourning. Following that tragedy I became very reluctant to travel by boat after hearing about that accident, but a few years ago, I had travelled to Bequia for the first time with some family members just to enjoy the beach and sightseeing.

The morning we embarked the big ship at Kingstown harbour, I went on the top deck to admire the views of the Island and the sea. When I looked down, the sea water was bottle green colour. You bet, I knew then it's a colour I associate with depth and the sea looked very deep. The Caribbean Sea is the World's fifth largest body of water.

I remember thinking the boat looked solid and seaworthy, but I was still a bit nervous when it sailed off to Bequia. The captain advised me to travel on the top deck, and it was a calm journey out to Bequia, but on the return journey, the wind had picked up and the ride was like a seesaw. I felt the urge to pray for our safe return to dry land.

When we arrived in Kingstown after an hour on the rough sea, I knelt and thanked God we were back on dry land. My grandma often told me "*cowards die many times before their deaths*". That saying made a lot of sense to me.

Chapter 6

Neighbours

Good Neighbours Are The Golden Thread
That Ties All Hearts Together

Great-uncle Harold was terminally ill, and I often visited him at his bedside with Mammy Darling, who was his sister. I was only five years old, but I vaguely remember he called me crayfish; he was referring to my complexion. It is typical in our culture to distinguish between different shades of black skin. Uncle Harold was married to Tina (Nennie Browne) and had three children—son Wilmot and two daughters Delta and Almaida.

The late Wilmot was deaf and he used sign language. One day, I went to the local shop for him. I bought him tinned sardines, and when I returned from the shop, I knew the minute I saw his face that I'd misinterpreted his request, so he waved me on in a disappointed manner. At the time, I felt so guilty and upset. It remains a mystery what he wanted me to purchase for him.

Marjorie was Nennie Browne's stepdaughter, and she was a few years older than I was. She had a hard time living with her stepmother. She was not allowed to play while the other children played. She did all the chores. In later years, Marjorie migrated to Trinidad with her mother, and many years after that, she was killed in a road accident in Trinidad. God rest her soul.

Nennie Browne attended evening service regularly after she joined a new religion from Curacao, a Pentecostal religion called Streams of Power. Nennie Browne joined the new Streams of Power Church, and we used to attend the night service with her.

One night, on our way back from church, we approached a place where a man by the name of Kitchilo lived; he had been murdered a few days earlier by a local watchman. As we walked past the gate, my younger cousin Laverne remarked, "Um um me kar smell shit."

You can picture the scene: four innocent children walking with Nennie Browne on a dark night. Apparently, we were supposed to walk by quietly. The old folks believed that when you were out at night, any bad smell in the air had something to do with the presence of a ghost. Nennie Browne was convinced it was Kitchilo's ghost. She said to Laverne, "*me know if nobody na say nooum yo go say something*". (I knew you would say something.)

Forgive Everyone Everything . . .

Our neighbour Isabella kept dried powdered milk to make tea and coffee. Every day, she noticed the milk was getting less and less, even though she was the only person using it. She asked her husband if he had used the milk, and he denied it. She decided to carry out her own detective work to find out who the culprit was and she poured farine into the powdered milk. Later that night, her husband sat in his chair eating something crunchy. Problem solved. Farine is made from cassava, a starchy vegetable that was grated and sun dried, and we ate it as a crunchy cereal.

In later years, when Isabella's husband had passed away, she met a man and he came to live with her. He told neighbours his name was Moving Cloud. It was an appropriate name for him as he was a fugitive running from the law. As soon as news got to him that policemen were coming, he disappeared, and Isabella never saw Moving Cloud again.

Mother Welch was a dark-skinned old lady who lived next door to Mammy Darling. She had many children who lived locally, and one of her daughters had migrated to Trinidad. Mother Welch was a good neighbour, but very loud and aggressive when provoked. She rowed with quite a few people, with the exception of Mammy Darling.

Grandma was too quiet and respectable to argue with neighbours. I learned the word *notorious* at a very young age from Mother Welch. When she argued with a young woman, she would often shout, "Yo notorious wretch; yo pussy dry like a biscuit." Even at a young age, I remembered thinking how does she know that? I later realised they were just hurtful words.

Mother Welch's son David lived at Mt. Bentic (Georgetown), and she often visited her son. I think in those days they walked all the way to Georgetown (about six miles) and back, so by the time she arrived home in Chapman's Village, it was pitch dark. Sometimes if it had rained heavily, as she approached my grandma's yard, she often shouted, "*Darling me come back, David send howdy*", and one evening I heard her scream loudly, "Ta ta ta ta," when she spotted a big frog (cropo), especially sometimes if a frog jumped high and landed on her foot.

It was common to see big frogs scrambling out of their dry holes. When it rained heavily, they would rush out into the dirt roads. Even though these creatures are good swimmers, hundreds of frogs and snails (konoo-quarter) came out from their dry holes to escape floods. I imagine it was easier for them to crawl on wet soil. The konno-quarters looked like small turtles; the only difference was that their bodies looked soft and spongy and above the eyes, they had a pair of antennas that expanded. It was a slimy creature. It was normal to see konoo-quarters on our way to school, crawling across the dirt pathways on early, dewy mornings before the sun started to heat up. By the time I was old enough to run about, all of Mother Welch's children had left home. She lived with two of her grandchildren—Clifford and Goody. Clifford and Goody were much older than I was, and as soon as they were old enough, they left home to live with their partners.

Goody went to live at a neighbour's home with her boyfriend, who came from Biabou village. He used to wash his condoms to reuse them. He often hung them to dry where we could reach them. At the time, we thought they were balloons and blew them up. Goody and her boyfriend didn't suspect it was us, we were too young to know any better.

Shortly after, Mother Welch fell ill. Her daughter Henrietta, who lived in Trinidad, returned home to care for her. Henrietta knew me, but I didn't remember her, as I was a baby at the time when she migrated to Trinidad. She was a beautiful, dark-skinned woman with lovely, flawless skin, and she always dressed immaculately and wore bright red lipstick.

Auntie Cynthia lived in Trinidad, too, so Henrietta and Auntie often sat on the doorstep reminiscing about life in Trinidad. I loved to listen to them talk about San Fernando and Port-of-Spain, and I thought their whiney Trinidadian accent was the best way to speak. Henrietta became my hairdresser and styled my hair using iron combs she heated on an open fire. It was a long process. I had to sit very still to avoid getting my scalp or ears burnt, and even sitting still, I got burnt.

It was not a pleasant experience, but it was a minor sacrifice to pay for a hairstyle.

The iron combs were placed on hot coals in a coal pot to heat up, and Henrietta separated small strands of my hair and used the hot comb to straighten it bit by bit, until my entire head of hair was straightened. After styling, I had to take extra care not to get it wet, or the hairstyle would be short lived.

A neighbour who lived on a hill above us was a fisherman and every evening he sold the fish he caught to neighbours. Mr Onhill spoke in a thick, regional accent, different from the local accent we were accustomed to hearing, and people used to mock him. Everyone made fun of him because he often told his wife when she was preparing dinner that she should knead the dumplings tight, tight.

In those days, quite a few local men went to America to pick fruit, and one of Mr Onhill's sons spent six months in America. When he returned he spoke in a thick American accent, and consequently, people named him Yankee. I thought at the time it was amazing that after spending a short time in another country, his accent could suddenly change.

In the mid-afternoons, while children played outdoors, some of the frisky adult neighbours used to sneak indoors to have sex. There were no locks on the bedroom doors, and some bedrooms only had curtains partitioning them off from the living room. My sister, cousins, and I often caught couples in compromising situation when we crept indoors.

In retrospect, being confronted with adult behaviour didn't ruin my childhood innocence. In fact, I think as a teenager it helped me understand that there are two types of relationships. For example, people caught in the act were not affectionate, and they didn't show me anything I should emulate. In my view, a meaningful act of love should be affectionate.

I realised it was simply two people behaving in a brutish manner, and it gave me the impression it wasn't act of love. Later on, when I saw the two people together, it was impossible to link them as romantic partners. On reflection, it was just two people acting out an obsession without commitment. Our grandmothers often told me that relationships without commitment could result in unwanted pregnancies. They often talked about young women having babies they couldn't afford to raise.

The other type of relationship is long term, committed, and meaningful, found normally between married or unmarried couples. I learned this important lesson, and my definitive conclusion back then was that I wanted a relationship like my grandparents. Furthermore, our grandparents were devoted Christians, and they showed so much respect to each other. They were role models who instilled good guidelines.

I'd learned decorum and self-discipline, and the decision to set high standards for myself was fundamental. My advice to teenagers, girls and boys: "*The moment you settle for less than you deserve, you get even less than you settled for*". In life, I would advise all teenagers to set high standards and believe in yourself. When you take care of your reputation, you earn greater respect from others. Always believe in better, and that you are special and unique.

Kind Deeds Are Good Memories

On a few occasions, it was common to see crazy women walked around the village stark naked and bewildered. A crazy lady by the name of Elfreda lived next door to my grandparents. She spent many years in a mental hospital and was released when I was about ten years old. Elfreda was no threat to anyone, but I was mischievous and often used to shout "manicoo," a nickname that people gave her. Every day, she stood in her yard shouting and arguing alone. This was amusing to me, and I often watched her talking to herself it was a one woman comedy show. First, she would ask a question and then shouted her answer out loudly. It was a two-way conversation, and I thought it was hilarious. I later learned Elfreda had a mental disorder known as schizophrenia.

A lady who lived in New Grounds often travelled to Chapman's Village in search of Nurse Browne because she thought my Mum could help cure her mental condition. One early morning, when I was getting ready for school, my grandma was braiding my hair. As the lady entered the yard, Mammy Darling told me to stay indoors.

I peeped through the window in shocked horror and saw the crazy woman with mad eyes looking at Mammy Darling. Grandma stayed calm as she tried to explain to the crazy woman that my Mum was not at home. Thank God, she calmly left the yard and went her way. How weird and wonderful was this lady? When she was good, she was one of our lunchtime caterers at school.

She sold delicious muffins, salt fish cakes, and peanut sugar cakes. As the Vinci saying goes, "*Wey na kill a fatten*," and I am living testimony. When the lady was good, she was very, very, good, and when she was ill we had to make do with mauby and bread or cake for our school lunch. Ah well, I have drunk stale mauby on many occasions for my school lunch.

A man named crazy Rory travelled from Diamond village, where he lived, looking for Mammy Darling, who people reckon resembled crazy Rory's wife. To this day, I don't know if his wife had died or if they were separated. One day, crazy Rory came to my grandma's house, and we had a big mirror hanging in the living room. Crazy Rory looked in the mirror and he went wild in a rage.

I made my escape through the back door. We were lucky he had calmed down within minutes, but Mammy Darling was hiding far away in the garden until he left. Luckily, we could see people approaching our home ahead, so Mammy Darling often had enough time to hide before crazy Rory arrived at the front gate.

Perfect—Is Not A Natural Human Trait

Young Merle was mentally ill, and one day she ended up at New Grounds village, a long way from her home. We had just finished school for the day, and all the schoolchildren started following and taunting her, but I suppose it's typical when you are a certain age.

Her clothes were torn and dirty, she had no shoes on her feet, and the tarmac road was very hot at that time of day. She travelled through the village with the school crowd from New Grounds to Chapman's, the same direction we were heading to go home.

When we arrived at my friend Jackie's home, her mum was very kind and gave crazy Merle something to eat. After that, I felt guilty and ashamed for the way we had treated her and realised we were doing a terrible thing. I decided to stop. Merle was just ten years old, the same age as us, but she was unable to attend school because of her illness. She just roamed the villages. People often teased her and treated her like a freak.

My friend's mum helped me to understand that we all need to be tolerant. I am grateful for the lesson I'd learned. We are not all perfect. *"perfect is not natural"*. It is a human trait to be imperfect. We must show kindness to everyone, as no one knows what the future brings, and if I experience misfortune, I want to be treated with tolerance and respect.

Chapter 7

School

Personality Is Good For Opening Doors,
But Its Character That Keeps It Going

At five years of age, I started infant school at New Grounds. The building was adjacent to the Methodist Church, which housed the primary school on weekdays. I can even remember the names of some of my teachers at infant school—Miss Clerke, a brown-skinned Indian lady, Miss Spencer (Auntie Venus) and Miss Forbes. I'd learned the alphabet with pictures as follows:

A for Apple	J—Jug	S—Saw
B—Bat	K—King	T—Tent
C—Cat	L—Lamp	U—Umbrella
D—Dog	M—Mother	V—Van
E—Egg	N—Nail	W—Window
F—Fish	O—Orange	X—Xylophone
G—Gate	P—Pen	Y—York
H—House	Q—Queen	Z—Zebra
I—Ink	R—Rake	

Every day, our class used to recite the alphabet. It was written on the black board a catchy verse and I quickly learned my ABC. In those days, pre-school education was mainly for children from rich families, so all other children started school with the same level of knowledge.

We recited numbers one through to ten as follows:

One, two	—	Buckle my shoe
Three, four	—	Shut the door
Five, six	—	Pick up sticks
Seven, eight	—	Lay them straight
Nine, ten	—	A big fat hen

I remember coming home from school starving hungry and my grandma often prepared sugar cane; it was peeled and sliced for me to eat before supper was ready. On other days, she made juice from limes, oranges, or lemons and sugar; these were all delicious drinks with no preservatives.

We had a big orange tree in the garden right next to the house, and I looked forward to when the orange tree was laden with ripe, juicy oranges. I often climbed the tree with a little penknife and collected oranges in my pocket, and then found a comfortable spot to sit in the tree and feast. I ate as many oranges as I could, not realising at the time that it was a good source of vitamin C.

Our infant school was a separate building adjacent to the big church, and the government provided milk and nutritional biscuits for us. The biscuits were kept in the church vestry and they were nice snacks for the teachers, too. The primary school housed grades one through sixth class. The smaller infant school classes housed beginners through to stage three, and at that stage, I was bright enough to move to class two, so I skipped class one.

When I was about seven years old, our teacher took us outside to play a game about once a week. Our class formed a circle, and the game was about a farmer who picked a wife (one of the girls) and then picked children to make up a family. One day, when we were playing the game, the teacher picked a boy to be the farmer. The farmer stood in the middle of the circle and the other pupils sang the lyrics as follows:

The farmer in the dell
The farmer in the dell
Hi-ho, the derry-o
The farmer in the dell
The farmer takes a wife
The farmer takes a wife
Hi-ho, the derry-o
The farmer takes a wife
The wife takes a child (2x)
Hi-ho, the derry-o
The wife takes a child
The child takes a nurse (2x) . . .
The nurse takes a cow (2x) . . .
The cow takes a dog (2x) . . .
The dog takes a cat (2x) . . .
The cat takes a rat (2x) . . .
The rat takes the cheese (2x) . . .
The cheese stands alone (2x)
Hi-Ho, the derry-o
The cheese stands alone

The farmer picked a wife, and the scabby boy who was playing the farmer picked me as his wife. I remember how irritating it was that of all the girls in our class he had to pick me. Then the wife took a child, and so on, until there was a whole family. The scabby boy suffered from eczema, and all my schoolmates scorned him. In retrospect, it was cruel and demeaning of us. May the good Lord forgive me!

We played a game with our teacher, and the pupils of five to seven year olds asked the following questions:

"Mr. Wolf, Mr. Wolf, what is the time? One o'clock," and the entire class followed the teacher, who played Mr. Wolf, and we repeated the questions until Mr. Wolf answered that the time was (dinnertime) twelve o'clock.

This game was recreational and educational, as we learned to focus on the moment our teacher shouted dinnertime. In fact, as we approached the twelve o'clock mark, we had to scarper, and the unlucky person the teacher grabbed was out of the game.

I remember the adrenaline rush and surge of excitement after we recited the ten o'clock verse. We had to be ready and alert to escape Mr. Wolf grabbing us for dinnertime at twelve o'clock. It was a fun game for my friends and me.

To Be In Good Time, Is A Necessary Rule

I think it would be fair to describe my time at New Grounds Primary School as a strict disciplinarian period, but I still managed to have fun. Depending on the mood our headmaster was in, if we arrived late to school and the big green door was closed, we knew we were in trouble. The only entrance to class was through the other door, where our headmaster stood at the top of the stairs with a leather belt.

We were orderly; late pupils formed a line, and one by one we stretched our hand out to be punished by a lash with the leather belt. It was terrifying for me, as my grandparents didn't believe in physical beatings. I remember the stinging pain and my hand going bright red and sore. We had two options: to stretch our hand out or be lashed on our backs. Neither was pleasant. Sometimes my grandma would confront the cruel man on her way to the women's league meeting, but I suppose it was the school rule of the day, in fact grin and bear it.

In Class 2, I had to learn poems, and each pupil took turns reciting the poems in front of the 'class. Each lesson lasted an hour. During that lesson, I was eager for the hour to pass so that my turn to recite the poem was missed; sometimes it did, but you bet your life the next lesson the teacher would continue the recitation from where she left off. The person who was missed in the last lesson would commence that lesson, and I never got away with it. Some of my classmates told me that when I had to learn poems, I should put the book under my pillow at night to help me remember the verses in class. They believed that if I slept with the book under my pillow I would remember everything I had revised for an exam. I now realised this was nonsense.

My schoolmates also told me that if I pinched the skin on one of my knuckles and it stayed up for a while, it meant I would pass my exams. Again, this is nonsense.

My primary school days were not all fun and frolic. One day, I was ordered to write one hundred lines because I arrived late to school. It had such a lasting effect on me I can still remember the sentence to this day: "*To be in good time is a necessary rule*". In those days, an exercise book was about fifty pages thick, so we often kept an exercise book specifically for detention and line writing. We learned to use two pens by holding them together to write out our lines. I just held two pens and wrote the lines in half the time.

"Every day after lunchtime, the whole school recited a prayer:

> *We thank the Lord for this our food,*
> *But most because of Jesus Christ*
> *Let manna to our souls be given,*
> *The bread of life sent down from heaven".* Amen!

We had lunchtime for an hour from 12:00-13:00 o'clock.

I remember every Thursday after lunchtime at 13:00 o'clock the entire Primary school used to participate in singing lesson for an hour. One of the songs I recall as follows:

> *"Grey sand and white sand*
> *Who will buy my white sand(x2)*
> *Who will buy my grey sand(x2)*
> *Grey sand and white sand"*

One by one each class began singing in turns after the first chorus line ended, then the next class began singing until the entire school sang the same chorus consecutively. From class 1 through to class 6 they sang out amazing soulful melodies. After our singing lesson ended it felt almost like therapy, and I felt calm and relaxed.

Arithmetic was not my favourite subject in school. I hated it with a passion. Teacher Mercury taught us decimal point calculations in Class 3, and I couldn't understand the technique. I was punished more than once when I produced incorrect work. Barbara (rest in peace, my friend) helped me. After she had explained the technique in "*kids' language*"—the language I could comprehend, all of my sums were correct, and I wasn't punished anymore. The beatings stopped, thanks to Barbara.

New Grounds Primary School received an invitation to a singing competition held in Kingstown by several school choirs participating. I was in the choir and after school, our music teacher conducted rehearsals. The song chosen was "Waltzing Matilda." I believe it originated in Australia. On the big day, we arrived at the Russell Theatre in Kingstown, and I was amazed to see pupils from Kingstown schools all smartly dressed in uniforms. The pupils from my school wore white dresses and the boys wore white shirts and khaki trousers. In those days, only a few of us wore uniforms to school as it was not complusory at New Grounds primary school.

On our way home from the competition, our bus drove through Sion Hill. The views from Sion Hill overlooking Kingstown at night were luminous. One of my friends who had never travelled to Kingstown at night saw the illumination and said, "Wa light" (look at lights) to explain the dazzling panoramic views of Kingstown shopping centre and harbour.

Children can be very cruel everyone laughed at my friend for being a country girl who had never seen Kingstown illumination.

I often played a joke with younger kids in the school playground. It was a magic game about two birds. I stuck two pieces of paper on my index fingers, and one sticker was designated as "Peter" and the other as "Paul." Then I used the middle finger next to the index finger without the sticker to indicate Peter had flown away. Then I repeated the same verse for Paul as follows:-

> *"Two little black birds;*
> *Sat on a wall;*
> *One name Peter;*
> *One name Paul;*
> *Fly away, Peter;*
> *Fly away, Paul;*

I bent the index fingers replaced the fingers with the middle finger without a sticker. It was amazing. No one noticed the switch. The final verse:

> *Come back, Peter;*
> *Come back, Paul"*!

Bring back the index fingers with the stickers; it's a great game for kindergarten kids. We played funny jokes on the playground with our school friends, especially younger kids who weren't aware of the outcome of the joke. I would lead while the other person would answer: Poo . . . A—C.

Ma . . . . *Poo(A)*
Ma . . . . *Poo(B)*
Ma . . . . *Poo*(C)

Life Is Drawing Without An Eraser

My school days at New Grounds were not without gloom, such as followed the sudden death of a friend. This had happened twice when I attended New Grounds School. I needed to come to terms with the reality of death and the mysteries of life, and this morbid experience pushed me to another level. It helped me to evolve maturity. I recall the day my grandma told me that life is a three-way process. We are born, we live, we die; truth is, life is fragile.

One of my school friends fell from a moving tractor belonging to the local estate. He sustained internal injuries unbeknown to his family, and a few days later, he was in a serious condition, but by the time he was admitted to the hospital, it was too late to save him. This was a very sad time for all at New Grounds primary school, and it was the first time I understood that life is unpredictable.

There was another tragic road accident. The young victim was in his late teens and from a nearby village. Apparently, he was travelling on his bicycle when he collided with a bus. He died from his injuries. I went to his funeral, and when his sister lamented that she had just ironed his shirts when the accident happened, I felt her pain.

A school friend's father met his death in a freak accident. A tree he was chopping down fell on his leg. His leg was badly broken, and he passed away in the hospital from the injuries he suffered. Some weeks later, we were on our way to school, as we got near our friend's home, we called out for her to walk to school with us. As clear as a bell, we heard her deceased father answered, *"Jane na da home"* (Jane is not at home). We all looked at each other, shocked and amazed. The voice was clear and concise, so it wasn't one mind playing tricks; we all heard the same thing, and we ran as fast as we could to school.

Tribute to Our Pet Dog, Sparrow

We had a little black and gold bull puppy from our Uncle Jack. We named the puppy Sparrow. It was only a few months old. One evening, Sparrow was playing in the garden, and it chased and bit a frog. Unfortunately, frogs can secrete a poisonous, milky liquid, and our puppy swallowed some of it. We looked on helplessly and watched our puppy froth at the mouth and died almost instantly.

Polly and I were distraught. We stood on the doorsteps in shocked disbelief. We started to cry, and granddad was surprised that the little puppy would have such a devastating effect. The next morning, my sister and I went with granddad to the bottom of the garden, and he buried Sparrow in a big, brown, crocus bag. We sprinkled purple forget-me-not flowers on the grave.

Experience Is An Amazing Lesson, It Teaches You
To Recognise A Mistake When You Make It Again

We attended the occasional evening theatrical show (tea meeting), and people participated in singing competitions and comedy acts at New Grounds School. Our aunts agreed that children must learn to be confident, so they decided to teach my cousin and me a song so we could enter the competition. Aunt Nita often talked about tea meeting nights and she won a goat as first prize several times for reciting poems. My cousin and I entered the show, and the rule was for us to sing consecutive lines of the song:

There's a hole in my bucket,
Dear Liza, dear Liza;
There's a hole in my bucket,
Dear Liza, a hole.
And why don't you mend it,
Dear Liza, dear Liza?
And why don't you mend it,
Dear Liza, dear Liza? Mend it!

My cousin and I were just ten years old, and it was one of our most humiliating moments. We actually went up on stage with a plastic bucket and sang our hearts out. I recall how embarrassed we felt, hence the reason I chose not to disclose my cousin's name. I prefer to keep her anonymous.

Emmanuel High School—Kingstown

The Best Vitamin For Making Friends Is . . . (B-One)

I started Emmanuel High School in Kingstown at the age of twelve years. The school building was just around the corner from the Kingstown General Hospital. During the summertime school break, shortly before I started secondary school, the building was burnt to a shell and a new building was found just above the juicy beverage factory and the Mac Connie supermarket in Kingstown.

My school days at Emmanuel High were absolute joy. For our uniform, we wore white blouses, bottle green pleated skirts, green and white ties, bottle green socks, black shoes, and a straw hats. Every day, we had to walk more than two miles from home setting out at 7am to the main road in San Souci (New Grounds gap) to catch our school bus. The school bus driver who lived three miles away had to travel the opposite direction to collect us and then a return journey towards Kingstown.

A few children from the nearby village at Lowman's Windward travelled in the same school bus, but they were picked up from outside their homes about a mile from the main road en route to Kingstown.

The class divide was obvious back then, and we were from poorer families, so we had to walk to the main road a few miles from home to catch a ride to school, even though we were charged the same travel fares. It was only in severe weather, such as heavy rainstorms, that we got a ride straight to our home; otherwise, we were dropped off at the nearest main road. Travelling to school every day was fun nevertheless.

I used to look forward to break time at school, as the ice cream factory was just a short distance away. The De Nobriga ice cream parlor employed a number of staff that rode bicycle carts around Kingstown selling ice cream and the ice cream man used to park outside our school gate during break times. There were many flavours of ice cream to choose from, sold in little tubs and choc ice on sticks. My favourite ice-lolly was soursop. The other flavours of ice cream were vanilla, chocolate, coconut, strawberry, and various fruity ice-lollies.

At lunchtime, we used to walk to the Hadaway store at Middle Street to purchase lunch for a dollar. It was a medium bread roll filled with delicious ham from a big tin container imported from America. We ate the ham sandwich with a bottle of juicy beverage for lunch. In retrospect, a medium bread roll with ham and mustard and a bottle of fizzy drink was just a snack. After school, I felt very hungry as most days our calorific intake was way below normal requirements, and the hot sun sapped all my energy.

During my time at secondary school, Kingstown was a rainbow colours of students dressed smartly in school uniform. Everyone attended school looking very smart and tidy. Girls' High School students wore navy blue skirts, white blouses, navy blue ties, navy socks, black shoes, and a straw hat. The Grammar School for Boys students wore khaki uniforms, and the school building was adjacent to the Girls High School. Intermediate High School students also wore navy blue uniforms.

Bishops College Secondary School students wore maroon skirts and ties, white blouses, and girls wore a straw hat. The boys wore white shirts, maroon ties, and khaki trousers. A short distance away from Bishops College was the Convent High School for Girls.

They wore light blue skirts with a big square pleat to the front and back, white blouses, and white socks with plimsolls. Similarly, St Martins' Secondary School for Boys students wore white shirts, black narrow ties, and black trousers.

Every summer, all secondary schools in Kingstown participated in competitive sports at Victoria Park. The relay race in the hot Caribbean sun was not my forte, and I was grateful it was just an annual event. We had some highly competitive students from Emmanuel High School, and we won quite a few trophies for the relay races, but I take no credit as I was not one of the competitive students.

In a way, travelling by school bus with students from other schools presented an excellent opportunity for us to socialise. It was beneficial for our personal development. My first romantic encounter was a student from St Martins' Secondary School for Boys, but I was still very naive at the time.

We did silly things as we travelled home on the school bus. I often carried his school tie home with me. He trusted me to return it the next morning. I suppose this was his way of wooing me with his charms. Auntie Cynthia discovered the tie one evening, and I had to lie to her. Oh yes, my flamboyant courtship was short lived, but in my opinion, this was because I wasn't ready for romantic relationship.

A Smile Is The Same In Every Language

The late Dr. Eustace, principal and founder of Emmanuel High Schools, Kingstown and Mesopotamia, was a tall, light skinned stocky man. His wife, a Canadian, ran the school bookshop in Kingstown and his sister Ruth Eustace was my scripture teacher. His daughter Grace was a teacher at Emmanuel High School in Mesopotamia. Dr. Eustace used to act as a substitute to teach a class on behalf of an absent teacher. One day he was teaching our class of twelve-year-olds in form two. He always enjoyed telling funny jokes; he was a bit of a comedian. He told us that an English man was admitted to the Kingstown hospital unconscious, and the next day when he woke up, he asked the nurse; *"Did I come here to die"*? The nurse thought he said *"today,"* and she replied, *"No, yesterday"*.

Dr. Eustace thought it was funny and he laughed at his own joke, but to his disappointment, we didn't understand the joke, so we didn't find it funny. The entire class stayed silent.

One day, I was misbehaving in class, and my English teacher shouted, *"Annice, little things amuse little minds"*. The teacher in question also told our class that he liked to eat burnt rice; after that, we gave him an appropriate nickname: "Bonbon."

Teacher Williams

~*~*~*~*~
Tribute
~*~*~*~*~

Teacher Williams was a young buoyant man who had just completed teachers' training in the late Sixties when he started his career at Emmanuel High School.

Teacher Williams was my French teacher, a tall, well-built man. I recall how he used to walk with his head held high. He was a commander. He entered the classroom and said, "Bonjour, la class", and the class responded, "Bonjour, Teacher Williams". He controlled our class with vigour and efficiency. Teacher Williams loved to play the guitar, and he sang "*lemon tree very pretty*" at a concert. This song will always remind me of him.

Gone, but not forgotten. God rest your soul.

School Holidays

The big break from school was in August when fruits were in abundance, the weather was nice, and we went to the beach. Our Great-uncle Samuel lived next door. Some of the mangoes in Uncle Sammy's garden had weird names, for example, Horsey and Feelings they were juicy and sweet though. He picked fresh coconuts, and we drank coconut water and ate coconut jelly harvested from his garden. I remember Uncle Sammy cooked enough food to feed five people, and during the day when our Gran was too busy to prepare a hot meal, we went to his house for lunch. He often cooked casseroles with yams, and dumplings with beef or pig tails. It was a hot, delicious meal for us.

Picnic on the Beach

On school holidays at least once a week, we spent half the day at the beach. On some occasions, it was an organised school trip. The local beach was just half an hour's walk, and we carried beach balls and packed lunch in our picnic basket—corned beef or sardine sandwiches and several fizzy juicy drinks. The juice drinks were our favourite drinks when I was growing up, and my favourite flavor was grape juice. The other flavours were orange, banana, and cherry. There are edible grapes (bay side grapes) growing by the seaside in St Vincent, and coconut trees, so we had access to coconut water or coconut jelly and picked grapes—natural snacks readily available on the beach.

Some people carried pilau rice and chicken, or macaroni and cheese. On some occasions, we carried breadfruit, we made a big wood fire with bits of dried coconut shells, and roasted the breadfruit. We used to dip the roasted breadfruit in seawater, which gave it a salty flavor. We used to scrape the burnt ashes off the breadfruit and cut them into small slices.

Sometimes we ate them with smoked herring or salt fish and drank beverage juice or mauby. My grandparents told me the bitter/sweet taste of mauby was good for the blood, and I think the mauby drink is an acquired taste. You liked it or loathed it.

We bathed in salty seawater; mixed with hot sun, it quickly turned the skin very dark. It made our skin peeled the next day. I have never felt comfortable walking in the hot sun, and I always felt the urge to wear a hat to protect my face and head. But we had no idea how damaging the sun was to the skin.

Every school holidays we visited our Great-aunt Elma; she lived at Fairhall, about ten miles away from our home. We travelled by General bus, and alighted at Calliaqua, by the main road. Aunt Elma's house was about a mile away towards Fairhall. It was a perilous journey, as the road was covered with gravel stones. It was uncomfortable for Polly and me, as we wore flip-flop sandals.

En route to Fairhall, we passed a mental hospital, and we often met mental patients who were well enough to go on errands. Gran told us they were from the hospital, and I was extremely nervous when we met them. The mental hospital was located a short distance from the main road. I saw naked patients sitting on the windowsill overlooking the road. They couldn't get out because the windows had heavy iron bars, but I was very young, and I didn't understand that I wasn't in any danger.

When we approached the mental hospital, I felt very nervous and often held Gran's hand tightly. Some of the patients waved at us excitedly. Gran said, "*look, that one is waving*", but I couldn't look. I thought the patients were demons, and I was absolutely petrified of them.

Aunt Elma worked at a big estate. It was the biggest house I had ever seen and slept in. My sister and I looked forward to our visits to Fairhall. Oh, it was grandeur—the house was surrounded by a big garden with well-cut green lawns and a huge stretch of flat land adorned with mangoes, oranges, tangerines, several varieties of plum, sapodillas, sweetsops—nearly every tropical fruit trees you could think of was on that stretch of land. To my sister and me, it was paradise. We ate as many plums and mangoes as we could in one day. It was a taste of the good life for certain. This was the first home in which I had seen a Christmas tree.

Chapter 8

Church

Cleanliness Is Next To Godliness

Early on Sunday mornings before breakfast, I used to go to the local bakery. Grandma always requested two large salt and sweet bread. On my way back from the bakery, I couldn't resist the delicious sweet, sticky, glazed bread. I used to pick the doughy part of the sweet bread. When I arrived home, I couldn't hide the fact that I had eaten quite a bit of it. As punishment, grandma would say I'd had my share and I could not have no more of the sweet bread.

On a typical Sunday morning, Mammy Darling woke early to cook lunch before going to church. The meal was normally pork, chicken, or beef with rice and peas. Mr Humphrey was our local butcher, and he lived next door to Great-uncle Malcolm. Every Saturday, he blew a big seashell to alert villagers that he had fresh meat for sale. Grandma bought fresh meat from Mr. Humphrey for our Sunday dinner regularly.

The church building was a thirty-minute walk to New Grounds, the same building in which we attended primary school on weekdays. The minister conducted church services on alternative weeks, and on the other Sundays, a local preacher conducted services.

When the local preacher conducted services, it was obvious as half of the church members stayed away, but when the minister conducted services, the church was at full capacity. My sister and I attended regular services, but by the time that I was ten years old, church for me was like a comedy sketch show.

It became a place where we misbehaved—whispering and giggling with friends. I was the busy body sitting in Church and looking for something to amuse me. As children hate to be constrained my sister and I couldn't sit quietly for over an hour, and the church atmosphere never worked for me. My sister and our friends found it difficult to sit attentively. It was a tall order to expect children to sit as still as adults and listen quietly. I was the main culprit, and I often looked for something to laugh about, in truth, I was one of the trouble makers and the leader of the pack in those good ole days.

One Sunday in church, my grandma whispered to one of my cousins, she said; "*close your mouth to avoid flies entering*". At the time, I thought it was hilarious. My little cousin always sat in church with his mouth open, oblivious of the fact that he was inviting pests. Mammy Darling often told us that we must always attend church service clean and tidy. She believed that a tidy appearance showed respect to our divine master. Furthermore, places of worship are for moments of quietness that can replenish the soul. It is the best place to go when you feel sad and lonely. I often sit in church and absorb the atmosphere even today when I need to gather strength. Try this; you would be amazed at how happy it can make you feel.

Mammy Darling was a choir lady at the New Grounds Methodist Church. Her weekly diary of church functions included regular mid-week women's league meetings. Depending on the time of year, she used to practice for special harvest church service. The women's league used to plan singing competitions and held the event at one of the regional churches in yearly sequence. As children needed to be supervised, grandma didn't think it appropriate to take us along with her, so we had to stay at home with one of our aunts.

God Always Gives His Best To Those
Who Leave The Choice With Him

It was most upsetting when grandma was making plans to travel by bus to the women's league singing competition. I often travelled with her everywhere. The event was held on a Sunday afternoon, but as soon as she left, I found something exciting to occupy my time. The minister at New Grounds church was a bald head man, and one day in church, I noticed he had a grey and white spot just above his forehead. Good heavens; I looked again and I saw it was bird droppings on his head. A bats nest was just above the pulpit. I suppose Satan was happy in our midst, and this was a classic time to ignite bad behaviour from me.

I whispered to my friend Joy, who was sitting right next to me, and I told her; "*bird shit inna e head*" (*He has bird mess on his head.*) Unaware, the Reverend continued to preach. My friend whispered to my sister, who sat next to her, and the news travelled fast down the church bench. By that time, laughter had taken control of me. It got so bad I had to go outside and composed myself.

My grandparents were busy concentrating on what the preacher had to say, and they probably thought I had gone to the toilet. After a few minutes, I returned to my seat and the minister eventually used his handkerchief to wipe away the mess. He had no idea of the fun we had; he was oblivious to the fact that we had seen it. During church communion, members from each pew took turns walking to the altar bread and communion wine. As a rule, members stood at the altar and formed a semi-circle in front of the minister. The incident between my friend Joy and I could only be put down to Satan working in our midst. We were on our way to the altar for communion, and I joined the queue from the left aisle of the congregation. Joy came from the right pew.

As we approached the altar, I stood next to her to form a semi-circle and the minister stood in front of us. We didn't speak, but just a glance and we began to giggle. The incident was heating up, and I saw Joy's throat wobbled as she tried to restrain herself. She was much better at suppressing laughter in church, but when I giggled, it made quiet a loud sound.

The minister came to us, he gave us a piece of bread, and said, "*The body of Christ*" by that time, we were both calm and collected, and when we took the tiny glass of wine, the minister said, "*The body of Christ; drink this in remembrance*". Joy and I were relieved, and I thanked God we didn't explode into uncontrolled laughter, so Satan didn't win. Joy and I often reminisce about that incident. She lives in America and I live in the UK, and we remain great friends.

The church grew to full capacity of dedicated members. People travelled from Diamond's and Lowman's Windward villages to attend services at New Grounds Methodist Church. My sister and I grew up in a religious and well-organised manner, and as the reverend repeatedly said in his prayers; "*I'm thankful*".

Rev. Thomas was my favourite minister at the time, even though we misbehaved in church. I felt his sermons were spiritual and uplifting, especially on communion Sundays. I believe preaching was his gift, and he conducted it with conviction. There were moments I would take time to listen to him pray, and I felt cleansed from my little sins. Sunday service lasted an hour, and the wooden benches were uncomfortable to sit on for long periods. One Sunday, a four-year-old girl turned to her mum and without hesitating she said; "*Mammy, the bench a squeeze me batty*". She spoke loud enough for us to hear. The child's innocence allowed her to speak what she saw and felt, and in order to avoid a repeat of the remark, the mother sat her daughter on her lap.

We often travelled home from church, sheltering under opened umbrellas to protect us from the mid-day scorching sun, and our grandfather and great uncle often stopped off at the rum shop. On our way home, we bought ice lollies (palettes) made with cherry juice and ice cubes to mix with a delicious fruit punch we had with our Sunday dinner.

After Sunday dinner, we went to Sunday school, and after Sunday school, the older girls would sometimes take a stroll with their boyfriends. We were allowed to stroll with them so that the old folks wouldn't suspect any wrongdoings.

A weird thing happened when an illiterate woman christened her baby son at New Grounds Methodist Church. There were three babies at the baptism service and the mothers and godparents gathered at the altar. When it was the illiterate woman's turn, the minister held her baby in his arms, he turned to her, and said; "*Name this child*". The woman replied; "*Lucifer*".

The minister was speechless. He couldn't believe what he had heard. I knew that the devil's name was Lucifer, as I had learned quite a bit of Bible stories at Sunday school. It was such an embarrassing thing to witness. My sister and friends couldn't control our giggles. I cannot recall whether the minister refused to name the child Lucifer. I believe he did, and this news created big gossip in our community.

Church service was the focal point of our social structure, and there were a few youth clubs for children to join. They held weekly meetings and organised day trips to meet with other clubs. The church organised special events, and members travelled to other islands. The youth club choices were the Red Cross Society, Four-H Club, Girl Guides, and Boys' Brigade.

On special Sundays, Easter, Harvest, and Christmas, all of the youth club members went on parade prior to the morning service. The parade took place outside the churchyard, and everyone attending service gathered as spectators. The Red Cross members wore white dresses with a red cross on the sleeve, Four-H Club members wore brown/green overalls, Girl Guides wore navy overalls, and the Boys' Brigade wore a uniform similar to the police academy.

On Sunday evenings, a few local women walked around the villages and sold homemade desserts. They carried the desserts on a big baking tray—it was slices of sweet potato pudding and various cakes. Other women sold parched peanuts or peanut cakes; it was similar to buying ice cream from an ice cream van.

Chapter 9

Special Occasions

Good Times Become Good Memories;
Bad Times Become Good Lessons

We enjoyed many special occasions from New Year's day into old year night. The last day of the year, we often stayed up late. Mammy Darling told us "*we should set up*" to see the old year out. As I grew older, I was able to stay awake and sat listening to the radio broadcasting events that happened throughout the year. In the last minute of the old year, a bell chimed, and the countdown began to bring in the New Year. One night, when I stayed up late with Mammy Darling, she said the wind was blowing strong outside and the old year was passing to bring in the New Year. At the time it was a serene moment, and I felt an eerie sensation.

At Easter time it was spiritually uplifting occasion in church. From Thursday (Holy Thursday) to the following Easter Monday was a special time for christians, and Methodist christians ate only fish for Easter Sunday main meal. We also ate hot cross buns with cheese, and grandma often made ginger beer. We could never eat hot cross buns without homemade ginger beer; they go so well together.

Church services began on Good Friday, and on Easter Sunday, the sermons were dedicated to the resurrection and remembrance of Christ. Everyone wore white to church at Easter. One of my favourite hymns at Easter was "*there is a green hill far away where Christ was crucified*".

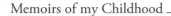

When I sang that song I used to imagine the Middle East, Jerusalem, from the pictures I'd seen in the Bible stories at Sunday school.

Easter

I recalled the moment of intense spiritual emotion for me. The Shakers (Pentecostal religion) conducted a big service that lasted all through Easter. It was a time when new members prior to Easter devoted forty days and nights of intense mourning. They knelt and prayed in a special sanctuary. During that period of holiness (forty days mourning) the converted members stayed in a special sanctuary. After that, new members were baptized, and during the service, each new member presented their testimony and gave an account to the congregation of the period they spent in sanctity.

At Easter the new church members took turns talking about his or her journey. My neighbour mother Welch, was a member of the Shakers, and I often attended the Easter service with her on Sunday evening. All members wore long white gowns with a touch of lilac or purple band around the waist. It was lively preaching, and members were overpowered into visionary aura while they spoke in tongues.

During the service an intense period of holiness, I found it astounding to listen as members sang, chanted, and were overwhelmed by emotions. It was incredible to watch. Some people slipped into trances and toppled over onto the floor. I believe members and non-members felt consecrated as they sang and prayed.

At Easter, the old folks believed that if you broke an egg in a glass of water and litmus paper and left it standing from sunrise for a few hours, the egg would predict your future by forming an appropriate shape. Some people recognised the shape of a ship, an airplane, or even a coffin. This was clearly not an experiment for the faint-hearted.

After Easter, we looked forward to summer break in August our longest school holidays it was free time, free time. I spent most of my summer breaks with my other grandparents and played all day with Polly. Sometimes I stayed overnight or all week until Saturday evening. Then Polly and I would go over to grandma after she came home from shopping in Kingstown. We always enjoyed the special treats she bought.

On a May Day bank holiday, there was a competitive sports day in our village. It is the only one I can remember at that time. There were relay races for the children and one game for the men to challenge. They had to climb a greasy pole. The most agile men in the village, one by one, tried to climb the greasy pole to the top. The pole was covered with something they called talla grease. It was very sticky, and it was impossible to climb to the top. None of the men managed to climb the greasy pole, but it was hilarious to watch them try.

Carnival

A few months before carnival celebrations began in July, a radio program broadcasted a competitive event held to pick a calypso king and queen for the new carnival year. That year, the names of the calypso king and queen were the Mighty Sparrow and Calypso Rose. One of the calypso songs by the Mighty Sparrow was "*Melda oh yo making wedding plans*", and it was the first year we were allowed to go to Kingstown carnival procession in 1968. Prior to carnival day, dance hall celebrations were held at the village hall, and the men playing the steel band drove around in an open truck and pre-rehearsed their music to invite villagers. When I heard the wonderful melody I wished that I were old enough to go to the fete.

Carnival was a three-day event, and it was a scary time for me. I was petrified of people playing masquerade. They dressed up in costumes and walked around the village with their faces covered and only their eyes were visible. It was weird even though I could guess who the masquerade was as it was normally someone from the village.

I was still petrified it was one of my phobias. The masquerade played a game carrying a shoebox. The shoebox contained a frog or a lizard and the mystery was to guess what was in the box. Most kids were petrified of masquerades, and I was no exception. We often hid indoors until everything was calm again.

Carnival is a public holiday in St Vincent, and it is a big street party. Each island has its own special music festivals. I went to my first carnival in 1968 in Kingstown, and the road march at the time was by the Mighty Sparrow. *"Carnival in 68, Mama, this one go be great"*. Another song was *"Archie broke them up"*.

I heard a young girl singing, adding her own rude lyrics to the song. My sister and I joined the procession. I was excited and looked forward to our day of fun. The street was closed to traffic, and revelers gathered from Grenville Street, where the bacchanal began.

We chose a calypso band to follow from Grenville Street and the crowd matched right down to Victoria Park. About six o'clock, when most revelers were intoxicated with strong rum, our aunt told us it was time to leave town. People were getting unruly, and the men began breaking bottles to use as weapons when the fighting broke out.

Some of the calypso lyrics were clearly not for children to repeat, and if we sang any of the rude lyrics, our grandparents told us off. I think I used to irritate my sister as I often tried to entertain her by playing steel band music verbally. It irritated her back then, but today she reminisces with pleasure.

The Mighty Sparrow and Bob Marley will always be known as the Caribbean calypso and reggae music kings.

Statehood Celebrations—October

A few months before St Vincent and the Grenadines Statehood celebrations were held in October 1969, we had learned a new anthem in school. Two verses would stay in my memory forever: the Lord's Prayer, and the national anthem of St Vincent and the Grenadines. They cannot be erased. Therefore, I would like to congratulate (better late than never) the composer of our Vinci anthem for the comprehensive lyrics, in my opinion, they are meaningful words that combine the Isles of St Vincent and the Grenadines. The anthem as follows:-

> "Saint Vincent . . . Land so beautiful,
> With joyful hearts we pledge to thee
> Our loyalty and love, and vow
> To keep you ever free.
> Whate'er the future brings,
> Our faith will see us through.
> May peace reign from shore to shore,
> And God bless and keep us true.
>
> Hairoun! Our fair and blessed Isle,
> Your mountains high, so clear and green,
> Are home to me, though I may stray,
> A haven, calm, serene.
> Our little sister islands are
> Those gems, the lovely Grenadines,
> Upon their seas and golden sands
> The sunshine ever beams."

At the time, I felt very proud of my birthplace. However, I didn't understand the political aspects for the Statehood celebrations, but I knew it would be historical. Gran thought it would be a memorable occasion, so she arranged for Polly and me to attend the Statehood celebrations in town. It was my first glitzy night out. The Statehood celebrations were held at Victoria Park in Kingstown. We stayed overnight with family who lived nearby at Frenches in Kingstown.

Prime Minister Milton Cato addressed the audience; although his performance was a memorable event, I wasn't interested in his long speech. I was more interested in the refreshments on sale. My favourite drink at the time was a milky chocolate drink. It was a chilled bottled drink, and it tasted similar to a chocolate milkshake.

Prime Minister Cato's eloquent speech gained many enthusiastic supporters, as it was broadcasted over the radio for the whole country to listen to. The political forum had changed from dull rhetoric by the former prime minister to a more robust term by PM Cato. After the speech and all of the pleasantries, a fireworks display adorned the night sky with rainbow lights in various patterns. I had never seen anything like it before, and I thought it was wonderful.

Our grandparents voted Labour, and for a few months during election campaign, people couldn't speak openly about the party they were supporting. The two main parties were the People's Political Party (PPP) and the Labour Party (LP), symbolised by a clock and a star, respectively. My grandparents warned us not to wear a star because they thought it was too dangerous. It was democracy at its worst, as our grandparents were worried that opposition supporters could attack us with a machete.

Sky Rocket Night—November

On November 5 (Guy Fawkes Night in the UK), we call it skyrocket night in St Vincent. Mammy Darling bought us sparklers from town. As soon as it got dark, our skyrocket celebrations began. We were very excited and all gathered round grandma. She lit our sparklers, and we ran from our house to our neighbour's until the sparklers burnt out.

It was customary on skyrocket night for people to celebrate in street procession in the evening. Later on, I sat indoors listening to villagers sang their favourite calypso songs and played drums and mouth organs (harmonica). They travelled through the villages carrying old car tyres, attached to a metal chain, which they set alight, and pulled along behind them.

We were not allowed out, but the next morning, on our way to school, we saw where the burning tyres had left a trail along the tarmac roads. Mammy Darling told us it was too dangerous to be walking around with tyres alight, but we saw the remains of a night of fun.

All Souls Night In St Vincent

"Jumbies (Ghosts) Let Go Tonight"

Halloween night is known as *"All-Souls Night"* in St Vincent, and it is a nostalgic reminder of my childhood. At that stage in my life, I learned to be petrified of dark nights. In fact, the old folks used to warn us that *"jumbies let go tonight"* on the remembrance night. It was traditional for families of dead relatives to lit candles on graves. On that special night I conjured up scary fantasies that filled my mind with eerie emotions.

It was on that remembrance night when I saw the cemetery at a distance it had hundreds of burning candles twinkling in the dark. I'd imagined the ghosts were out from their graves because of what the old folks told us. Besides, I thought all the jumbies that came out from their graves were outside, lurking in the dark. That was a fearful time for me late at night when we sat indoors.

A few decades later, Michael Jackson made a video of the same thoughts I had as a child. *Thriller* was exactly the way I imagined it to be on All-Souls Night in St Vincent when the old folks told me that *"jumbies let go tonight"*. Oh no, I didn't think jumbies were dancing outdoors like it was in Michael Jackson video, but I thought the jumbies were coming to get me.

You Reap What You Sow

At harvest time in November, farmers used to gather yams, sweet potatoes, dasheens, and all types of peas from their lands. It was traditional that during harvest time there would be a special service of thanksgiving for the bountiful crops. My sister and I looked forward to that Sunday. It was a celebratory time. Prior to the big day, grandma always prepared for us to wear new clothes and shoes. One harvest Sunday, I was dressed up like a celebrity. I can even remember the new dress I wore. It was a yellow and white flowery dress, and I wore a black shiny pair of shoes with a lovely white hat and white ribbons tied into bows at the end of my braided hair.

It was common to see dead frogs by the roadside. En route to church on Harvest Sunday, we normally saw many dead frogs, dried and flattened by vehicles. As I skipped along, I stepped right onto a dead frog and kicked it ahead of me. My sister and cousins had a good laugh at my expense. At Harvest service, Polly was the star in our family. She recited her poem in front of the congregation with such eloquence that the whole family felt proud of her. Whenever I recited a poem in front of an audience, I was very nervous. My body shook, I mumbled words, and I couldn't match my sister's standards. Polly participated more frequently at Church events. I didn't recite poems as often, but I was content with that decision.

It was traditional at harvest time for the minister to bless the produce members brought to church, and after service, they held a fete, selling goods, cakes and vegetables. There were various refreshments on sale, and I looked forward to our treat, especially homemade ice cream.

In those days, ice cream was prepared in a wooden bucket with handles that churned the custard mixture. I think they used, milk, sugar, vanilla, and crushed ice. That original taste set the standard, and I often compare modern ice cream to the ice cream I had in my childhood. I believe it was the best ice cream I'd ever tasted, but that's only my opinion.

Grandma didn't eat eggs, but she ate cakes. At Christmas, she used to spend the whole day preparing to bake cakes and bread. Prior to adding the ingredients to make cakes, grandma poured water into a big bowl, added the butter, mixed, and stirred it for at least an hour. She told me it was to get rid of the saltiness in the butter. Also, it increased the amount and made the butter light and creamy. One of her cousins Godfred Harry was a baker, and at Christmas, grandma used his big oven to bake her bread and cakes.

Grandma made everything from memory. My only regret I had kept no record of the recipes for the cakes she made. On Christmas morning, breakfast was normally very special. We had ham with homemade bread, and the ham was a big leg of pork sold at Christmastime. Our Christmas lunch was plentiful, and grandma often made delicious soursop juice. This drink had a consistency similar to vanilla milkshake and tasted just as delicious.

Christmas in St Vincent was not as commercial as in the UK, but we got a few toys that our family bought us, balloons, and a flute. However, when I was eight years old, we received gifts from England. On one occasion, I received a dolly and beach ball so whenever we went to the beach we played volleyball.

I remember one Christmas day, Polly and I went to Great-uncle Jack's house. Auntie Leah gave us red wine and black cake, a traditional Christmas treat in St Vincent. I took a sip of the wine, and it tasted of alcohol. I remember spluttering the strong taste, and the wine had sprayed the clean white tablecloth. I quickly turned the tablecloth so that the wine stain would be hidden away from Auntie Leah at least until Polly and I went home. I think I was about ten, and being so young, I got away with it as we weren't high on the suspect list, Auntie Leah didn't blame us for the wine stain on her lovely tablecloth.

We often saw men staggering home from the rum shops on Christmas day after they drank strong rum. One day my sister and I were on our way home from visiting Aunt Gladys when Polly saw a drunken man approaching us. I was petrified of old drunken men because they often carried a cutlass and behaved rowdily. Drunken men also had demented looks when we met them, walking and staggering along the dirt track. There was never any news of drunken men harming anyone, but it was one of my fears.

Weddings

A Kiss Is The Upper Affection For A Lower Invasion

A typical Vinci wedding took months to organise and make plans for the big day. The bridal party had to select colours and fabrics for bridesmaid dresses. It was team effort. Some ladies sewed the dresses, while others sewed sequins, and the bride and bridesmaids needed to make several trips to the dressmaker's home to fit and alter dresses accordingly.

Just a few days before the big event, the women in charge of catering got together to bake cakes and cook delicious meals. In my opinion, the most memorable time after the wedding ceremony was when the cars left church and travelled to the reception. Several cars following the bride and groom honked their car horns to mark the occasion and congratulated the newly wedded couple. All of the neighbours came out by the roadside to catch a glimpse of the newlyweds and wish them well.

It's a Vincentian tradition to decorate the entrance gate at the venue where a wedding ceremony was held. The entrance gate was decorated with an evergreen sago tree branch. The green leaves were designed into lovely, entwined plaits. It was a creative display built into an arch at the entrance to the wedding reception.

My most treasured delight was cousin Delta's wedding cake. It had white icing with some edible tiny silver and pink balls. It was the first time I had seen cakes with edible decorations. Mammy Darling told us not to feed the dog wedding cake, as the old folks believed it was bad luck if a dog ate wedding cake. They believed if a dog ate wedding cake the marriage would end in divorce.

Chapter 10

Recommendation

Education Provides Opportunities;
Christianity Gives Us Hope

I know from personal experience that parenting is not an easy role. In terms of parenting it is our behaviour and ability that determines how well we can cope when circumstances present good or bad situations. I believe that if parents and guardians set high standards, most of what you achieve will be reflected in the child you raise. The greatest credential for parenting is the ability to provide emotional and social intelligence to a young and impressionable child.

In my opinion, children who attend regular church service and Sunday school learn humility, compassion, and respect. I believe faith in God transforms lives. The lessons of any religion teach direction and routine. I got the impression from an early age that Sunday was a special day of rest in St Vincent.

On the first day of the week, we gave thanks to God in Church. I grew up with the notion that Sunday prayers would guide and protect me through the week. Every Saturday in our home, we prepared everything that we needed for Sunday. Grandma used to sort out clothes to attend church as well as prepare Sunday dinner. It was carried out with regimented precision every Saturday.

Never Give Up On Your Dreams

Looking back on my childhood, I honestly believe poor families brought up in a christian home developed better social skills than those who didn't attend regular church service and Sunday school. The difference between poor and rich families, children develop social skills in a more privileged environment. For instance, rich families can afford to take children on holidays abroad, and as a result, they mingle with different cultures and this exposure helps children to develop social skills. Whereas children in poor families can only develop social skills through school and church events. I believe it is imperative to set that balance with education and religion. When I was growing up children who attended regular church events benefitted more socially.

Moreover, I believe in terms of our ability we are all born with our own unique talent 'our gift' some of us are lucky to recognise and develop that gift. We often use the expression "gifted" to describe someone who does something efficiently. Some people may be excellent in an academic role. Others may demonstrate talent in careers as inventors, or in careers that demand practical, hands-on skills. In my culture, we tend to focus more on academic skills, and we believe it's the only way forward to achieve success. In my opinion, we need to broaden our minds think of the diversity of many talents that could accomplish success. In some instances, parents, peer groups, and teachers ignore or ridicule the less academic students. Consequently, these children feel worthless and undervalued by those who should be supporting them. I urge everyone, especially parents and teachers, to identify children who are not studious. Help them develop their creative or practical talents—in other words, their unique and gifted talent.

I remember schoolchildren who were slow learners would be stigmatised and often teased; even their families treated them differently. This is a prejudice we need to address. We should focus on diversity and help children to develop their unique talents. A child's hobbies and interests should always be encouraged. Instead of simply forcing children who are not studious to further literacy skills. We need to identify and encourage a child's full potential whether it be as an inventor or hands-on skill.

When they do not show any potential in academic subjects, we should not give up on them. I believe it is possible to control one's own destiny to some extent if he or she chose the right path in life. It is important for parents and teachers to identify the unique talent in children so that they can develop into resourceful independent adults.

It is true that progress has little to do with speed, but much to do with direction. The right direction and choice in life brings success. When you recognise your 'gifted talent' in any venture, the mid-stage is challenging, but after that, with perseverance success is just around the corner. Whatever career path you chose, nothing is too great to conquer. Anything is possible with determination. Focus on what you start with the end in mind, and replenish your energy to do your best. Keep striving for more. You can accomplish success.

My advice is to focus on what you are good at doing start low and aim high, teenagers you should . . . follow your dreams!

Chapter 11

Conclusion

"Kind Words Can Be Short And Easy To Speak,
But Their Echoes Are Truly Endless" (Mother Theresa)

I believe childhood builds a foundation that creates our personalities. Children are learners; they mimic what they see and hear. Therefore, it is important to encourage and congratulate a child for doing something good. Be aware that for good behaviour, we should praise children constantly. Give more praises and less criticism. This is important during a child's formative years to develop confidence. There is no such thing as one hundred percent good parenting, but as guardians, we can all relate to some shortcomings in that role.

Some children can test the patience of a Saint, but a little forbearance is the best way forward. As a child, I often heard grownups say, *"speak when spoken to, and do not interrupt adult conversations"*. As a result I used to sit in class at school thinking I must not interrupt my teacher. It was normal for adults to say, *"you talk too much"* to children who were talkative. I believe this verbal attack on a child can cause irrevocable shyness that extends into adulthood.

A young child needs to practice speaking to improve his or her vocabulary. Telling a talkative child to *"shut yo mout"* can severely limit how well a child communicates. It is better to allow children to talk freely, even if you share no interest in what they have to say. Give them a chance to speak it is for practical and personal skills.

Children often copy what they see and hear, whether it is good or bad. It is important to discipline children when they are naughty, but it is equally important to explain why you've shouted at or beat a child. At an early age, each child should understand who is in control they should recognise boundaries and show respect to elders. In short, show respect to earn respect; there is no age barrier to this rule. I urge parents, guardians, to never punish a child without explaining the reasons for your actions. More notably, discipline should not be something a child is fearful of.

Use subtlety and politeness to reprimand a child. It is also important to offer more compliments to children. I have learned that when you offer a compliment, it sends positive emotions to you and the recipient. When my daughters used to misbehave, I used my slipper to hit them. When I calmed down, I felt ashamed and remorseful. I didn't understand how important it was to explain to my children how angry I felt at the time, but it wasn't total failure, as I often hugged and kissed my children.

We should all aspire to treat everyone with the same consideration and respect we want for ourselves. It has positive, long lasting effect. I also think it's amazing how a small word like "sorry" can mean so much. What's more, we also need to appreciate constructive criticism rather than view it as a belittling insult. Constructive criticism can be valuable; we should use it as a way to improve and work towards a better future.

It Is more Effective to Repair a Child than an Adult

The Heaviest Emotion I Can Carry Is A Grudge

When I was ten, some of my relatives constantly ridiculed me. The reason being the Caribbean sun flushed my brown skin and bleached my hair a foxy red which was unattractive to many people. Nevertheless, my grandparents always showed me affection and called me "sweet child." However, some of my relatives often talked about Mrs. Copley. She worked in one of the big stores in Kingstown. Apparently, my family thought I resembled her.

I had not met Mrs. Copley, so I had presumed she was ugly, and my family didn't realise how upsetting it was for me. Some decades later, we were sitting at home chatting, and when I explained how much it used to upset me when they called me Mrs. Copley, my family described her as "beautiful." They had apologised for the misunderstanding and pain they had caused me.

Some grownups used to say very hurtful things, and they were not aware of the consequences of ridiculing a young, impressionable child. Some adults didn't hesitate to criticise a child if they believed that child was ugly or thin, had natty hair, a big nose, or big lips. When my relatives called me Mrs. Copley, it was the manner in which they called me Mrs. Copley, mocking and taunting me, it was very hurtful. In spite of this, I believe that bad experience was beneficial. I have learned a very important lesson that I should not tease anyone because I am conscious of the negative impact. It's a form of bulling, and if a child is bullied, that pent-up anger will continue into adulthood.

Beauty Is Skin Deep

I believe beauty is inside and out, but true beauty comes from within. In my opinion, beauty is diverse; spread it wherever you go in life. It can be through laughter, a smile or hug, or a handshake or a wave. All of these are happy gestures. I have also learned that it is better to adopt a simple approach to life, as this brings optimism and positive energy, both of which generate happiness:

> *If you love life, life will love you back;*
> *Wherever you go, take your whole heart along;*
> *Believe that your life is worth living and your beliefs will help*
> *create the fact.*

The community that I grew up in was not ideal, our lives lacked modern amenities. However, children could play freely in our neighbourhood, and we used to travel alone to fetch water from a nearby river. We kept our childhood innocence intact. Children today have access to television and the internet. When I was growing up, we didn't have access to modern technology. Ignorance was bliss. Besides during my childhood I was happy and contented we were imaginative and created our own play time activities.

The lessons I've learned from my upbringing equipped me with resourcefulness. For a short time during my formative years, the coal pot was the only domestic appliance on which my family could cook a meal. It was a challenge, and building a fire on which to cook a meal every day was an arduous task.

Finally, I believe it is imperative for us to be aware that in life there's no such thing as perfection, but in striving for perfection, we can achieve excellence. What's more, I have learned that to be happy in life means you should leave it to others to be perfect, to be wonderful, and to remain level headed, even when you achieve great things.

I am forever grateful for the way my grandparents nurtured me while Mum and Dad worked for a better life in England:

> *When I felt abandoned, they gave me: Protection . . .*
> *When I felt alone, they gave me: Affection . . .*
> *When I felt lost, they gave me: Hope . . .*

God Bless all Readers . . .

Glossary

Inna: *In*

Pickney yo go get bad blessing: *God would punish you my child*

Me bin fo: *I went to*

Wid: *with*

Fo piece a cocoa: *For a piece of cocoa*

E full a pepper: *It is full of pepper*

Yo lie yo na war fo gimme: *You are lying because you do not want to give it to me*

E catcha: *It caught*

Yo mum garn up inna car: *Your mum was seen in a car*

Do-ku-na: *Sweet potato pudding*

Wey na kill a fatten: *Whatever doesn't kill you really does make you stronger*

Oh, lard Doso stick on e kar move: *Oh, Lord; Doso is stuck*

Yo talk too much: *You're too talkative*

Shut yo mout: *Be quiet*

Um, um, me kar: *No, no, I could*